TOURISM INTERRUPTED

THE IMPACT OF COMMUNICABLE DISEASES ON TRAVEL TRENDS

PROF. (DR.) NITISH BHATIA

Dedicated to Our Families

Contents

Preface

Travel and tourism have become essential parts of our globalized world, bringing economic growth and cultural exchange. However, alongside these benefits, communicable diseases have repeatedly disrupted these activities throughout history. From ancient pandemics like the Bubonic Plague to modern outbreaks such as SARS and COVID-19, diseases have profoundly affected how we travel, trade, and interact.

This book, "Tourism Interrupted: The Impact of Communicable Diseases on Travel Trends," explores how diseases have shaped travel patterns and impacted economies. It dives into historical outbreaks that altered trade routes, changed pilgrimage routes, and influenced societies. It also examines recent outbreaks, showing how they challenge healthcare systems, influence crisis responses, and change how people travel and plan trips.

Each chapter provides a detailed look at specific disease outbreaks, explaining where they started, how they spread, efforts to stop them, and the effects on economies and societies. By studying these past events and current challenges, we hope to learn how to better handle future health crises that affect global travel.

Through careful research and analysis, this book aims to help governments, healthcare professionals, tourism businesses, and travelers understand the risks and strengths of the tourism industry when facing infectious diseases. By understanding these dynamics, we can better prepare for and manage the impacts of diseases on travel and tourism.

As our world continues to connect more closely, understanding the balance between health safety and global travel becomes increasingly important. "Tourism Interrupted" takes readers on a journey through history and current events, offering insights into how diseases have shaped and continue to influence our travels and daily lives.

Prof. (Dr.) Nitish Bhatia Pune

R. Rishi Venkat July 2024

Acknowledgements

We extend our heartfelt gratitude to the School of Pharmacy and the Department of Travel and Tourism at Vishwakarma University, Pune, whose support and encouragement were instrumental in the creation of this book, "Tourism Interrupted: The Impact of Communicable Diseases on Travel Trends."

We are deeply thankful to the faculty and staff members of Vishwakarma University for their invaluable guidance and assistance throughout this endeavor. Their expertise and dedication have been crucial in shaping the content and ensuring its relevance to both academia and industry.

A special mention goes to the Centre of Teaching and Learning (CTL) at Vishwakarma University. The Contemporary Curriculum Pedagogy and Practices (C2P2) activity organized by CTL provided the foundational framework that inspired and guided the research and writing of this book. We acknowledge with gratitude the innovative teaching methodologies and scholarly support provided by CTL, which have enriched our academic journey.

This book stands as a testament to the collaborative spirit and academic excellence fostered at Vishwakarma University. We are grateful for the opportunity to contribute to the fields of pharmacy, tourism, and public health through this comprehensive exploration of the impact of communicable diseases on global travel trends.

CHAPTER ONE

Understanding Communicable Diseases

Introduction

Communicable diseases, also known as infectious diseases, are illnesses caused by pathogens that can be transmitted from one person to another, from animals to humans, or through the environment. Understanding these diseases is crucial in assessing their impact on various aspects of human life, including travel and tourism. This chapter provides an overview of the definition, classification, modes of transmission, and historical perspectives on epidemics and pandemics.

1.1 Definition and Classification

Communicable diseases are caused by infectious agents such as bacteria, viruses, fungi, and parasites. These pathogens can invade and multiply within the human body, leading to illness. Communicable diseases are classified based on their causative agents and modes of transmission.

1.1.1 Bacteria

Bacterial infections are caused by pathogenic bacteria. These single-celled organisms can thrive in diverse environments, including soil, water, and the human body. Common bacterial diseases include:

- **Tuberculosis (TB)**: Caused by *Mycobacterium tuberculosis*, TB primarily affects the lungs but can spread to other organs. It spreads through airborne droplets when an infected person coughs or sneezes.
- **Cholera**: This acute diarrheal illness is caused by *Vibrio cholerae* and spreads through contaminated water or food. It is prevalent in areas with poor sanitation.
- **Typhoid Fever**: Caused by *Salmonella typhi*, typhoid fever spreads through contaminated food and water. Symptoms include high fever, fatigue, and abdominal pain.
- **Antibiotic Resistance**: Overuse and misuse of antibiotics have led to the emergence of antibiotic-resistant bacteria, posing a significant public health challenge.

1.1.2 Viruses

Viral infections are caused by viruses, which are smaller than bacteria and require a host cell to replicate. They can cause a range of illnesses, from mild to severe:

- **Influenza**: Commonly known as the flu, influenza is caused by influenza viruses and spreads through respiratory droplets. Seasonal flu outbreaks occur annually, and pandemics arise when new strains emerge.
- **HIV/AIDS**: Human Immunodeficiency Virus (HIV) attacks the immune system, leading to Acquired Immunodeficiency Syndrome (AIDS) if untreated. It spreads through blood, sexual contact, and from mother to child during childbirth or breastfeeding.
- **COVID-19**: Caused by the novel coronavirus SARS-CoV-2, COVID-19 emerged in late 2019 and rapidly spread worldwide. It primarily spreads through respiratory droplets and has caused significant global disruption.

- **Vaccines**: Vaccination is a key strategy in preventing viral infections. Vaccines stimulate the immune system to recognize and fight specific viruses.

1.1.3 Fungi

Fungal infections are caused by fungi, which can infect the skin, nails, and respiratory system:

- **Athlete's Foot**: A common fungal infection affecting the skin of the feet, caused by dermatophytes. It spreads through direct contact with contaminated surfaces.
- **Histoplasmosis**: This respiratory illness is caused by *Histoplasma capsulatum*, a fungus found in soil contaminated with bird or bat droppings. Inhalation of spores can lead to infection.
- **Candida Infections**: Candida fungi can cause infections in various parts of the body, including the mouth (thrush) and genital area (yeast infections). Immunocompromised individuals are particularly at risk.

1.1.4 Parasites

Parasitic infections are caused by organisms such as protozoa, helminths, and ectoparasites:

- **Malaria**: Caused by Plasmodium parasites transmitted by Anopheles mosquitoes, malaria is prevalent in tropical and subtropical regions. Symptoms include fever, chills, and anemia.
- **Giardiasis**: This intestinal infection is caused by the protozoan *Giardia lamblia* and spreads through contaminated water or food. Symptoms include diarrhea, abdominal cramps, and weight loss.
- **Schistosomiasis**: Also known as bilharzia, this disease is caused by parasitic worms (schistosomes) and spreads through contact with contaminated freshwater. It can cause chronic health problems if untreated.

1.2 Modes of Transmission

Communicable diseases spread through various modes of transmission, which determine how pathogens are passed from one host to another. Understanding these modes is essential for preventing and controlling outbreaks.

1.2.1 Direct Contact

Direct contact transmission occurs when there is physical contact between an infected individual and a susceptible host:

- **Touching**: Simple physical contact, such as shaking hands or hugging, can transmit diseases like impetigo and ringworm.
- **Kissing**: Close contact through kissing can spread diseases like mononucleosis (the "kissing disease") and herpes simplex virus.
- **Sexual Contact**: Sexually transmitted infections (STIs) such as HIV, syphilis, and gonorrhea spread through sexual contact.

1.2.2 Indirect Contact

Indirect contact transmission involves the transfer of pathogens via contaminated surfaces or objects:

- **Fomites**: Inanimate objects like doorknobs, utensils, and medical equipment can harbor pathogens. For example, norovirus can survive on surfaces and cause outbreaks in communal settings.
- **Shared Items**: Sharing personal items such as towels, razors, or needles can transmit infections like hepatitis B and C.

1.2.3 Droplet Transmission

Droplet transmission occurs when respiratory droplets containing pathogens are expelled from an infected person through coughing, sneezing, or talking:

- **Coughing and Sneezing**: Diseases like influenza, COVID-19, and pertussis (whooping cough) spread through droplets that can travel short distances and infect others nearby.

- **Talking and Singing**: Even speaking or singing can release droplets, posing a risk of transmission in close-contact settings.

1.2.4 Airborne Transmission

Airborne transmission involves the spread of pathogens through the air over longer distances:

- **Aerosols**: Pathogens can be suspended in the air as aerosols and inhaled by individuals far from the source. Tuberculosis and measles are examples of airborne diseases.
- **Ventilation Systems**: Poor ventilation can facilitate the spread of airborne pathogens in enclosed spaces, highlighting the importance of proper air circulation.

1.2.5 Vector-Borne Transmission

Vector-borne transmission involves the transfer of pathogens through vectors such as mosquitoes, ticks, and fleas:

- **Mosquitoes**: In addition to malaria, mosquitoes transmit diseases like dengue fever, Zika virus, and West Nile virus.
- **Ticks**: Ticks can transmit Lyme disease, Rocky Mountain spotted fever, and other tick-borne illnesses.
- **Fleas**: Fleas are vectors for diseases like plague, caused by Yersinia pestis.

1.2.6 Vertical Transmission

Vertical transmission occurs when pathogens are transmitted from a mother to her baby during pregnancy, childbirth, or breastfeeding:

- **Congenital Infections**: Diseases like syphilis and cytomegalovirus (CMV) can be transmitted to the fetus during pregnancy, leading to congenital infections.
- **Perinatal Transmission**: HIV and hepatitis B can be transmitted during childbirth or through breastfeeding, necessitating

preventive measures to protect newborns.

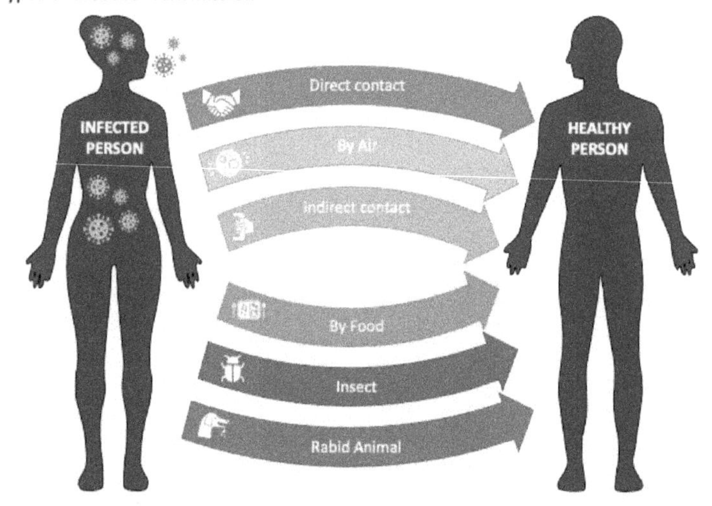

Modes of Transmission of Communicable Diseases

1.3 Historical Perspectives on Epidemics and Pandemics

Throughout history, epidemics and pandemics have had profound impacts on societies, economies, and cultures. Studying these events provides valuable insights into the challenges and responses associated with communicable diseases.

1.3.1 The Black Death

The Black Death, which struck Europe in the 14th century, was one of the deadliest pandemics in human history. Caused by the bacterium Yersinia pestis, it decimated the population and had lasting social and economic effects:

- **Spread and Mortality**: The plague spread rapidly through trade routes, including the Silk Road and maritime routes. It is estimated to have killed 30-60% of Europe's population.

- **Social Impact**: The massive loss of life led to labor shortages, economic upheaval, and changes in social structures. Fear and superstition influenced public responses, including the persecution of minority groups.
- **Economic Consequences**: The decline in population affected agriculture, trade, and urban development. Some regions experienced economic collapse, while others saw shifts in labor practices and wages.

1.3.2 The Spanish Flu

The Spanish Flu of 1918-1919 was an influenza pandemic that infected one-third of the global population and caused millions of deaths. Its rapid spread and high mortality rate highlighted the need for effective public health measures:

- **Global Impact**: The pandemic occurred in the final year of World War I, exacerbating its spread among military personnel and civilians. It killed an estimated 50 million people worldwide.
- **Public Health Response**: Measures such as quarantine, isolation, and the use of face masks were implemented, though often inconsistently. The pandemic underscored the importance of coordinated public health strategies.
- **Long-term Effects**: The Spanish Flu led to advancements in virology and epidemiology, laying the groundwork for future responses to influenza outbreaks.

1.3.3 HIV/AIDS Epidemic

Since its identification in the early 1980s, the HIV/AIDS epidemic has claimed millions of lives worldwide. The disease disproportionately affects certain populations and regions, underscoring the importance of targeted prevention and treatment efforts:

- **Epidemiology**: HIV/AIDS initially spread rapidly among specific groups, including men who have sex with men, intravenous drug users, and sex workers. It soon became a global health crisis.
- **Impact on Society**: HIV/AIDS has had profound social and economic impacts, particularly in Sub-Saharan Africa. The stigma associated with the disease has hindered prevention and treatment efforts.
- **Advancements in Treatment**: The development of antiretroviral therapy (ART) has transformed HIV from a fatal disease to a manageable chronic condition. Ongoing research aims to find a cure and improve prevention strategies.

1.3.4 Recent Pandemics

The 21st century has witnessed several significant outbreaks, including SARS, H1N1 influenza, Ebola, and COVID-19. These events have underscored the importance of global health security, rapid response, and international collaboration:

- **SARS (2002-2003)**: Severe Acute Respiratory Syndrome (SARS) was caused by a novel coronavirus and spread to over 30 countries. Swift public health measures, including isolation and travel restrictions, helped contain the outbreak.
- **H1N1 Influenza (2009)**: The H1N1 pandemic, also known as swine flu, emerged in 2009 and spread globally. Vaccination campaigns and public health interventions helped mitigate its impact.
- **Ebola Outbreak (2014-2016)**: The West African Ebola outbreak highlighted the need for robust health systems and international cooperation. Efforts to contain the virus included community engagement, quarantine, and the development of experimental treatments.
- **COVID-19 (2019-Present)**: The COVID-19 pandemic has had unprecedented global impacts, affecting every aspect of life. It has highlighted the importance of preparedness, surveillance,

and vaccine development.

Understanding the nature, classification, and transmission of communicable diseases is essential for comprehending their impact on travel and tourism. Historical perspectives on epidemics and pandemics provide context for the challenges and responses that shape our current approach to managing these diseases. As we move forward, lessons learned from past and recent outbreaks will continue to inform strategies for preventing and mitigating the impact of communicable diseases on global travel and tourism.

CHAPTER TWO

THE GLOBAL TRAVEL AND TOURISM INDUSTRY

Introduction

The travel and tourism industry is a dynamic and multifaceted sector that significantly contributes to global economic growth, cultural exchange, and employment. This chapter delves into the various components of the industry, its economic impact, key trends, and how global events, particularly communicable diseases, affect it. A thorough understanding of the industry provides context for assessing how disruptions can alter travel trends and the overall landscape of tourism.

2.1 Overview of the Industry

The travel and tourism industry comprises a wide array of services and sectors, each playing a vital role in facilitating travel and enriching the traveler experience.

2.1.1 Transportation

Transportation is essential for the movement of tourists, providing various options to suit different travel needs and preferences.

- **Air Travel:**

  - **Commercial Airlines:** These airlines offer scheduled flights, connecting major cities and countries. Airlines like Delta, Emirates, and Lufthansa serve millions of passengers annually.
  - **Low-Cost Carriers (LCCs):** Airlines such as Ryanair, Southwest, and AirAsia provide affordable travel options by cutting non-essential services, making air travel accessible to a broader population.
  - **Charter Flights:** These are non-scheduled flights typically used for package holidays, corporate travel, or special events, offering flexibility in departure times and destinations.

- **Rail Travel:**

  - **High-Speed Trains:** Countries like Japan (Shinkansen), France (TGV), and China (CRH) have advanced high-speed rail networks that offer efficient and comfortable long-distance travel.
  - **Regional and Commuter Trains:** These trains connect cities and rural areas, providing essential links for daily commuters and regional travelers.

- **Road Travel**:

  - **Buses and Coaches**: Services like Greyhound (USA), FlixBus (Europe), and RedBus (India) offer long-distance and intercity travel options.
  - **Car Rentals**: Companies such as Hertz, Enterprise, and Avis provide rental services for tourists needing personal transportation.
  - **Ride-Sharing**: Platforms like Uber and Lyft have revolutionized local travel, offering convenient and affordable transportation options.

- **Maritime Travel**:

  - **Cruise Ships**: Companies like Carnival, Royal Caribbean, and MSC Cruises offer vacation experiences that combine travel with leisure activities, visiting multiple destinations.
  - **Ferries**: Essential for connecting islands and coastal regions, ferry services are vital in countries like Greece, Indonesia, and the Philippines.

2.1.2 Accommodation

The accommodation sector offers diverse options to cater to different budgets and preferences, playing a crucial role in the tourism experience.

- **Hotels and Resorts**:

  - **Luxury Hotels**: Brands like Four Seasons, Ritz-Carlton, and Mandarin Oriental provide high-end services, including gourmet dining, spa treatments, and personalized services.
  - **Mid-Range Hotels**: Chains like Marriott, Hilton, and Holiday Inn offer comfortable and reliable lodging with a range of amenities.

- **Budget Hotels**: Brands like Ibis, Motel 6, and Premier Inn provide affordable options with basic amenities.

- **Vacation Rentals:**

  - **Platforms**: Airbnb, Vrbo, and Booking.com offer private homes, apartments, and unique stays, catering to travelers seeking a home-like environment or unique experiences.

- **Hostels:**

  - **Budget-Friendly Options**: Hostels like YHA, Generator, and HI Hostels provide dormitory-style and private rooms, often with communal spaces that encourage social interaction.

- **Camping and Glamping:**

  - **Outdoor Experiences**: Campsites in national parks and private campgrounds offer traditional camping, while glamping sites provide luxurious tents and cabins for a more comfortable outdoor experience.

2.1.3 Food and Beverage

Food and beverage services are integral to the travel experience, offering travelers a taste of local cuisine and dining experiences.

- **Restaurants:**

  - **Fine Dining**: Establishments like Michelin-starred restaurants offer gourmet cuisine and exceptional service, often showcasing local and seasonal ingredients.
  - **Casual Dining**: Family restaurants, diners, and cafes provide relaxed dining environments with diverse menus.

- **Cafes and Bars:**

- **Specialty Coffee Shops**: Chains like Starbucks and local cafes offer coffee and light snacks, often serving as social hubs.
- **Bars and Pubs**: These establishments offer beverages, including local and craft beers, wines, and cocktails, often with entertainment like live music or sports broadcasts.

- **Street Food**:

  - **Local Markets**: Street vendors and food stalls provide quick, affordable, and authentic meals, reflecting the local culture and culinary traditions.

2.1.4 Entertainment and Recreation

Entertainment and recreational activities enhance the tourism experience, offering a variety of options for leisure and adventure.

- **Cultural Attractions**:

  - **Museums and Galleries**: Institutions like the Louvre, the Smithsonian, and the British Museum offer insights into art, history, and culture.
  - **Historical Sites**: Landmarks like the Pyramids of Giza, the Colosseum, and the Great Wall of China attract tourists interested in history and heritage.

- **Natural Attractions**:

  - **National Parks**: Parks like Yellowstone, Kruger, and Banff provide opportunities for hiking, wildlife viewing, and experiencing natural beauty.
  - **Beaches and Islands**: Destinations like the Maldives, Hawaii, and the Caribbean are popular for their pristine beaches and water activities.

- **Theme Parks and Amusement Parks**:

- **Major Parks**: Parks like Disneyland, Universal Studios, and Six Flags offer a wide range of rides, shows, and themed attractions.

2.1.5 Travel Agencies and Tour Operators

These businesses facilitate and enhance the travel experience by providing planning, booking, and guided services.

- **Travel Agencies:**

  - **Full-Service Agencies**: Companies like American Express Travel and Flight Centre offer comprehensive travel planning, including flights, accommodations, and tours.
  - **Online Travel Agencies (OTAs)**: Platforms like Expedia, Booking.com, and TripAdvisor provide convenient online booking for flights, hotels, and activities.

- **Tour Operators:**

  - **Package Tours**: Operators like Trafalgar, Intrepid Travel, and G Adventures design and manage travel packages that include transportation, accommodation, and guided tours.
  - **Specialized Tours**: Companies offer niche tours focused on adventure, eco-tourism, culinary experiences, and more, catering to specific interests.

2.2 Economic Impact and Importance

The travel and tourism industry is a major economic driver, with significant contributions to GDP, employment, investment, and cultural exchange.

2.2.1 Contribution to GDP

The industry's contribution to GDP is multifaceted, including direct, indirect, and induced impacts.

- **Direct Contribution:**

- **Tourist Expenditures**: Spending on accommodation, transportation, food, and entertainment directly contributes to the economy.
- **Industry Value Added**: The value added by tourism-related industries, such as airlines, hotels, and travel agencies, is a direct contribution to GDP.

- **Indirect Contribution**:

  - **Supply Chain Activities**: Industries that supply goods and services to tourism businesses, such as food suppliers, construction companies, and technology providers, contribute indirectly.
  - **Government Spending**: Investment in tourism infrastructure and promotional activities by governments enhances the industry's capacity and attractiveness.

- **Induced Contribution**:

  - **Employee Spending**: Wages earned by employees in the tourism industry are spent on goods and services, stimulating further economic activity.

2.2.2 Employment Generation

Tourism is a significant source of employment, offering diverse job opportunities across various sectors.

- **Direct Employment**:

  - **Jobs in Tourism Businesses**: Positions in hotels, airlines, restaurants, and attractions directly related to tourism activities.
  - **Diverse Roles**: Employment ranges from frontline staff like receptionists and tour guides to management and administrative positions.

- **Indirect Employment:**

  - **Supporting Industries**: Jobs in industries that support tourism, such as food production, construction, and retail, are indirectly linked to tourism growth.

- **Seasonal and Part-Time Jobs:**

  - **Peak Seasons**: Seasonal tourism destinations, such as ski resorts and beach towns, offer temporary employment during peak travel periods.
  - **Flexibility**: Part-time jobs in the tourism sector provide opportunities for students, retirees, and those seeking supplementary income.

2.2.3 Investment and Infrastructure

Investment in tourism-related infrastructure is critical for supporting and sustaining the industry's growth.

- **Infrastructure Development:**

  - **Transportation Networks**: Building and upgrading airports, roads, and ports to improve accessibility and connectivity.
  - **Public Transport**: Enhancing public transportation systems to facilitate tourist movement within destinations.

- **Accommodation and Facilities:**

  - **New Developments**: Constructing new hotels, resorts, and recreational facilities to accommodate increasing tourist numbers.
  - **Upgrades and Renovations**: Investing in existing properties to improve quality and services.

- **Technology and Innovation:**

- ◦ **Digital Platforms**: Developing online booking systems, mobile apps, and virtual tours to enhance the customer experience.
- ◦ **Smart Tourism**: Implementing smart technologies, such as IoT, AI, and big data analytics, to optimize operations and personalize services.

2.2.4 Cultural Exchange and Diplomacy

Tourism fosters cultural exchange and international relations, promoting global understanding and cooperation.

- **Cultural Exchange**:

  - ◦ **Interpersonal Interaction**: Travelers and locals share traditions, customs, and knowledge, enriching cultural understanding and appreciation.
  - ◦ **Cultural Events**: Festivals, exhibitions, and performances allow tourists to experience and participate in local cultural activities.

- **Soft Power**:

  - ◦ **Nation Branding**: Tourism helps countries showcase their culture, history, and values, improving their global image and influence.
  - ◦ **Diplomatic Relations**: Tourism can strengthen diplomatic ties by promoting mutual understanding and cooperation between countries.

2.3 Key Trends and Statistics

The travel and tourism industry is continually evolving, shaped by emerging trends and statistical insights.

2.3.1 Growth in International Tourism

International tourism has seen remarkable growth, driven by various factors and highlighting key trends.

- **Rising Tourist Numbers:**

  - **Statistical Growth:** According to UNWTO, international tourist arrivals reached 1.5 billion in 2019, reflecting a consistent upward trend over the past decades.
  - **Travel Motivation:** Increased disposable income, improved transportation, and a desire for cultural and experiential travel are primary drivers.

- **Top Destinations:**

  - **Popular Countries:** France, Spain, the United States, and China consistently rank among the top destinations, attracting millions of tourists annually.
  - **Attractions and Experiences:** Iconic landmarks, cultural heritage, and unique experiences draw visitors to these destinations.

- **Emerging Markets:**

  - **Growing Destinations:** Countries in Asia (e.g., Thailand, Japan), the Middle East (e.g., UAE), and Africa (e.g., South Africa) are experiencing rapid tourism growth.
  - **Infrastructure Development:** Investments in tourism infrastructure and marketing campaigns are boosting these emerging markets.

2.3.2 Sustainable and Responsible Tourism

Sustainability and responsibility are becoming central to the travel and tourism industry, addressing environmental and social impacts.

- **Eco-Tourism:**

- **Nature-Based Travel**: Eco-tourism emphasizes environmentally responsible travel to natural areas, promoting conservation and minimal impact.
- **Conservation Efforts**: Eco-tourism initiatives often support wildlife conservation and habitat preservation, benefiting local ecosystems.

- **Community-Based Tourism**:

  - **Local Involvement**: This approach involves local communities in tourism planning and development, ensuring that tourism benefits are shared equitably.
  - **Cultural Preservation**: Community-based tourism helps preserve local cultures and traditions by involving residents in tourism activities.

- **Green Practices**:

  - **Sustainable Operations**: Tourism businesses are adopting green practices, such as reducing waste, conserving water, and using renewable energy.
  - **Certification Programs**: Programs like Green Globe and EarthCheck certify tourism businesses that meet sustainability standards.

2.3.3 Technological Advancements

Technology is transforming the travel and tourism industry, enhancing efficiency and the overall travel experience.

- **Online Booking and Digital Platforms**:

  - **Convenience and Accessibility**: Online travel agencies (OTAs) like Expedia and Booking.com make it easy for travelers to research and book trips.

- ○ **User Reviews and Recommendations**: Platforms like TripAdvisor provide user-generated reviews and recommendations, helping travelers make informed decisions.

- **Mobile Technology**:

  - ○ **Travel Apps**: Apps like Google Maps, Airbnb, and Skyscanner provide real-time information, navigation, and booking capabilities, enhancing convenience.
  - ○ **Contactless Services**: Mobile check-ins, digital boarding passes, and contactless payments improve safety and efficiency.

- **Artificial Intelligence and Big Data**:

  - ○ **Personalization**: AI and big data analytics enable personalized travel experiences by analyzing traveler preferences and behavior.
  - ○ **Operational Efficiency**: AI-powered chatbots, predictive maintenance, and demand forecasting improve customer service and operational efficiency.

2.3.4 Impact of Global Events

Global events can significantly impact the travel and tourism industry, leading to changes in travel behavior and industry practices.

- **Economic Crises**:

  - ○ **Reduced Travel Demand**: Economic downturns reduce disposable income and travel budgets, affecting tourism revenue and employment.
  - ○ **Recovery Strategies**: Post-crisis recovery strategies often involve government support, marketing campaigns, and

incentives to stimulate tourism.

- **Natural Disasters:**

  - **Disruption and Damage**: Natural disasters can disrupt travel plans, damage infrastructure, and lead to temporary declines in tourism.
  - **Resilience and Recovery**: Effective disaster management and recovery plans are essential for rebuilding and restoring tourism in affected areas.

- **Political Instability:**

  - **Safety Concerns**: Political unrest, conflicts, and terrorism can deter travelers from visiting affected regions, impacting tourism flows and safety perceptions.
  - **Diplomatic Efforts**: Governments and tourism organizations often engage in diplomatic efforts to restore confidence and attract tourists.

- **Pandemics:**

  - **Travel Restrictions**: Communicable diseases, such as the COVID-19 pandemic, lead to travel restrictions, reduced demand, and long-term changes in travel behavior.
  - **Health and Safety Measures**: Enhanced health and safety protocols, such as testing, vaccination, and hygiene measures, are implemented to ensure traveler safety.

The travel and tourism industry is a vital component of the global economy, with significant contributions to GDP, employment, investment, and cultural exchange. Understanding its structure, economic impact, key trends, and the influence of global events is essential for assessing the potential disruptions caused by communicable diseases. As we explore the historical and contemporary impacts of these diseases on travel and tourism, it is crucial to recognize the industry's resilience and capacity for adaptation in the face of challenges.

23

CHAPTER THREE

The Plague and Medieval Travel

Introduction

The Bubonic Plague, commonly referred to as the Black Death, was one of the most devastating pandemics in human history, ravaging Europe in the mid-14th century. This chapter delves into the mechanisms of the plague's spread, its immediate and prolonged effects on trade routes and urban centers, and its significant impact on religious pilgrimages. Through this detailed examination, we gain a comprehensive understanding of how a communicable disease can disrupt societies and alter historical trajectories.

3.1 Spread and Impact of the Bubonic Plague

3.1.1 Origins and Spread

Origins in Asia

The bacterium Yersinia pestis, the causative agent of the Bubonic Plague, is believed to have been endemic in rodent populations in the steppes of Central Asia, particularly around Mongolia. Genetic evidence and historical records suggest that this pathogen existed in these rodent reservoirs long before it caused human epidemics.

- **Endemic Reservoirs:** The central Asian steppes provided a perfect ecological niche for Yersinia pestis to persist among wild rodent populations, particularly marmots.

- **Silk Routes**: The interconnected trade routes, collectively known as the Silk Road, facilitated not only the exchange of goods but also the movement of pathogens. This vast network allowed Yersinia pestis to travel with merchant caravans and nomadic tribes, gradually spreading westward.

Introduction to Europe

In 1347, the plague arrived in Europe via Genoese trading ships that docked at the Sicilian port of Messina. These ships had traversed from the Black Sea, a crucial node in the Eurasian trade network.

- **Genoese Ships**: These ships carried infected rodents and fleas, which initiated the transmission cycle upon docking. Ports such as Venice, Genoa, and Marseille quickly became epicenters of the outbreak.
- **Black Sea Trade Hub**: The Crimea, particularly the city of Kaffa, was a pivotal trading hub where the plague may have been disseminated during a siege by Mongol forces, who allegedly catapulted plague-infected corpses into the city.

Transmission Mechanisms

The primary mode of transmission was through fleas that lived on black rats (Rattus rattus), which were prevalent in medieval towns and aboard ships. The bacterium could also spread through contact with bodily fluids or tissues of infected animals and humans.

- **Flea Vector**: Fleas, primarily Xenopsylla cheopis, would bite infected rats, ingest the bacterium, and subsequently bite humans, transmitting the infection.
- **Pneumonic Plague**: In cases where the bacterium infected the lungs, the resulting pneumonic plague could spread through respiratory droplets, facilitating human-to-human transmission.

Rapid Spread

The intricate network of trade routes and the high degree of mobility among merchants facilitated the plague's rapid dissemination across Europe.

- **European Spread**: By 1348, the plague had reached England, Scandinavia, and Eastern Europe, decimating populations along its path.
- **Beyond Europe**: The Middle East and North Africa also suffered from the plague, with major cities like Cairo and Damascus experiencing significant mortality.

3.1.2 Devastation and Mortality

High Mortality Rates

The lethality of the Bubonic Plague was unprecedented, with mortality rates estimated to be between 30% and 60% of the population in affected areas.

- **Contemporary Accounts**: Chroniclers of the time described streets filled with dead bodies and the near-total collapse of social order.
- **Regional Variations**: Some regions experienced higher mortality rates, which could exceed 75%, leading to the decimation of entire communities.

Devastation of Plague Pandemic

Demographic Collapse

The plague caused a profound demographic collapse, halting centuries of population growth and leading to a significant decline in Europe's population.

- **Population Decline**: Estimates suggest that Europe's population fell from approximately 75 million to around 50 million between 1347 and 1351.
- **Long-Term Effects**: The demographic impact was so severe that it took centuries for the population to recover to pre-plague levels.

Social and Economic Disruption

The dramatic reduction in population led to severe social and economic consequences.

- **Labor Shortages**: The death of a substantial portion of the workforce led to labor shortages, increased wages, and a shift in economic power from landowners to laborers.

- **Decline of Feudalism**: The feudal system began to erode as serfs and peasants demanded better conditions and pay, eventually leading to significant social and economic reforms.

Psychological Impact

The psychological toll of the plague was immense, leading to widespread fear, paranoia, and religious fervor.

- **Divine Retribution**: Many people interpreted the plague as divine punishment for sins, leading to an increase in religious penitence and the persecution of supposed heretics and scapegoats.
- **Mental Health**: The constant presence of death and the breakdown of societal norms led to widespread psychological trauma and a profound sense of despair.

3.1.3 Spread Mechanisms

Vector Transmission

The primary vectors for the Bubonic Plague were fleas that carried the Yersinia pestis bacterium.

- **Flea Biology**: Infected fleas would bite a host, regurgitating the bacterium into the bite wound. The bacterium could then spread to the host's lymphatic system, causing bubonic symptoms.
- **Rodent Hosts**: Black rats, which thrived in human settlements, were the primary hosts for the fleas, facilitating close contact with humans.

Human Transmission

The pneumonic form of the plague, which could develop from the bubonic form, allowed for direct human-to-human transmission.

- **Respiratory Droplets**: Infected individuals could spread the bacterium through coughing or sneezing, making close contact particularly dangerous.

- **Household Spread**: Entire households could be infected rapidly, leading to high mortality within families and communities.

Maritime and Overland Trade Routes

The extensive network of trade routes in medieval Europe played a crucial role in the spread of the plague.

- **Maritime Routes**: Merchant ships, carrying infected rats and fleas, spread the plague to port cities across the Mediterranean and beyond.
- **Overland Routes**: Trade caravans and travelers facilitated the inland spread of the disease, reaching even remote rural areas.

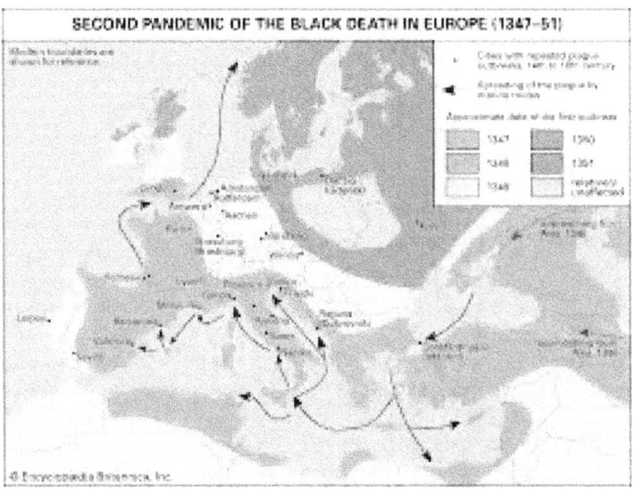

Route of Plague Pandemic Spread

Urban Density and Sanitation

The high population density and poor sanitation in medieval towns and cities created ideal conditions for the plague to thrive.

- **Overcrowded Living Conditions**: Overcrowded urban areas provided ample opportunities for the fleas to find new hosts among the human population.
- **Poor Sanitation**: Inadequate waste disposal and the prevalence of rats in cities exacerbated the spread of the disease.

3.2 Effects on Trade Routes and Urban Centers
3.2.1 Disruption of Trade Networks
Impact on Commerce

The fear of contagion led to significant disruptions in commerce as traders avoided plague-affected areas.

- **Trade Route Abandonment**: Many merchants ceased their activities, leading to shortages of essential goods and raw materials. This resulted in increased prices and economic instability.
- **Economic Recession**: The disruption of trade caused widespread economic recession, affecting both local economies and international trade networks.

Trade Embargoes and Quarantines

Cities and states implemented stringent measures to prevent the spread of the plague, including trade embargoes and quarantines.

- **Port Closures**: Many ports were closed to incoming ships suspected of carrying the plague, halting maritime trade.
- **Quarantine Measures**: Ships arriving from plague-affected areas were often quarantined for 40 days (quaranta giorni), a practice that became the basis for the term "quarantine."

Abandonment of Trade Fairs

Trade fairs, which were central to medieval commerce, saw declining attendance and, in many cases, were canceled.

- **Economic Hubs**: These fairs were crucial for the exchange of goods and services, and their decline had long-term economic consequences.
- **Cultural Exchange**: The fairs were also centers of cultural exchange, and their abandonment led to a reduction in the dissemination of new ideas and technologies.

3.2.2 Urban Decline and Migration

Urban Exodus

As the plague ravaged cities and towns, many people fled to the countryside to escape the disease.

- **Rural Migration**: The mass exodus to rural areas led to a significant decline in urban populations, leaving many cities depopulated and in disrepair.
- **Agricultural Impact**: The influx of urban dwellers into rural areas strained agricultural resources and disrupted rural economies.

Economic Contraction

The decline in urban populations and the disruptions to trade led to severe economic contraction.

- **Business Closures**: Many businesses closed due to the loss of workers and customers, leading to widespread unemployment and economic decline.
- **Market Decline**: Markets for goods and services shrank, further exacerbating the economic downturn.

Decline of Urban Culture

The cultural life of cities suffered as a result of the plague.

- **Arts and Education**: The loss of population and the general atmosphere of fear and despair impacted the arts, education, and religious activities. Many cultural institutions, such as universities and guilds, struggled to survive.

- **Social Fabric**: The social fabric of urban centers deteriorated as communities were decimated and social structures collapsed.

3.2.3 Social and Cultural Impact
Shift in Social Dynamics

The plague led to significant shifts in social dynamics and power structures.

- **Labor Power**: The reduction in population increased the bargaining power of peasants and laborers, leading to social unrest and demands for better wages and conditions.
- **Feudal Decline**: These shifts contributed to the decline of the feudal system as serfs and peasants gained more economic and social power.

Psychological Trauma

The psychological impact of the plague was immense.

- **Widespread Fear**: The constant presence of death and the collapse of social order led to widespread fear and paranoia.
- **Religious Fervor**: Many turned to religion for solace, leading to an increase in religious fervor and, in some cases, fanaticism.

Persecution and Scapegoating

In the chaos and fear that accompanied the plague, minority groups were often scapegoated and persecuted.

- **Anti-Semitic Pogroms**: Jewish communities were frequently blamed for the plague and faced pogroms and expulsions.
- **Witch Hunts**: Other marginalized groups, such as supposed witches, were also targeted as scapegoats, leading to persecution and violence.

3.3 Impact on Pilgrimages and Religious Travel

3.3.1 Disruption of Pilgrimages
Major Pilgrimage Routes

Major pilgrimage routes saw significantly reduced traffic due to the fear of contagion and the disruption of travel networks.

- **Camino de Santiago**: This famous pilgrimage route to the shrine of Saint James in Spain saw a dramatic decline in pilgrims.
- **Jerusalem and Rome**: Pilgrimages to Jerusalem and Rome were similarly affected, with many believers unable to undertake these journeys.

Impact on Religious Practices

The disruption of pilgrimages had a profound impact on religious practices.

- **Spiritual Crisis**: Pilgrims often undertook these journeys as acts of penance or devotion, and their inability to do so led to spiritual crises for many believers.
- **Religious Adaptations**: Religious communities adapted their practices to accommodate the disruption, including increased local devotions and the establishment of new religious sites.

3.3.2 Spiritual and Cultural Consequences
Spiritual Crisis

The plague triggered a widespread spiritual crisis, challenging religious beliefs and practices.

- **Divine Punishment**: Many saw the plague as divine punishment, leading to increased piety and religious fervor.
- **Church Authority**: The inability of the Church to protect people from the plague led to disillusionment and challenges to religious authority.

Cultural Adaptations

Religious communities adapted their rituals and practices in response to the plague.

- **New Devotions**: New prayers, saints, and religious devotions emerged, reflecting the people's desperation and hope for divine intervention.
- **Burial Practices**: Burial practices also changed, with mass graves becoming common due to the high death toll.

3.3.3 Legacy and Memory

Historical Remembrance

The Black Death left a lasting imprint on European memory, influencing art, literature, and cultural expressions.

- **Art and Literature**: Themes of mortality, suffering, and resilience became prominent in medieval and Renaissance art and literature.
- **Cultural Memory**: The collective memory of the plague influenced cultural and societal norms for generations.

Long-Term Societal Changes

The societal changes brought about by the plague had long-term consequences.

- **Feudal Decline**: The decline of feudalism and the rise of wage labor laid the groundwork for the transformations of the late medieval and early modern periods.
- **Economic Shifts**: The economic shifts that occurred due to the plague's impact on labor and trade networks influenced the development of modern economic systems.

The Bubonic Plague's impact on medieval travel, trade, and pilgrimage routes serves as a poignant reminder of how communicable diseases can reshape societies. By examining its spread, devastating mortality rates, and the resultant disruptions to trade networks, urban centers, and religious practices, we gain insights into historical responses to pandemics and their enduring legacies. Understanding these historical precedents informs our approach to managing and mitigating risks in contemporary global health crises, emphasizing resilience, adaptation, and collaborative efforts in safeguarding public health and sustaining tourism resilience.

CHAPTER FOUR

THE SPANISH FLU AND EARLY 20TH CENTURY TRAVEL

Introduction

The Spanish Flu, which erupted in 1918, was one of the deadliest pandemics in human history, resulting in the deaths of an estimated 50 million people worldwide. This chapter examines the global spread and mortality of the Spanish Flu, its impact on immigration, and the travel restrictions that were implemented in response to the pandemic. By exploring these facets, we gain insight into how this communicable disease influenced early 20th-century travel and shaped public health policies.

4.1 Global Spread and Mortality

4.1.1 Origins and Initial Outbreaks

Origins of the Spanish Flu

The exact origins of the Spanish Flu remain debated among historians and epidemiologists. However, it is generally believed to have originated in the United States, with some evidence pointing to a military camp in Kansas as the initial epicenter.

- **Haskell County, Kansas**: In early 1918, a local outbreak of severe influenza-like illness was reported among soldiers at

Camp Funston, part of Fort Riley in Kansas. The camp was a major training base for American troops being sent to Europe during World War I.

- **Military Movement**: The movement of troops between the United States and Europe facilitated the spread of the virus. Soldiers, often living in close quarters, were highly susceptible to infectious diseases, which could spread rapidly through military encampments.

Spread to Europe and Beyond

The virus quickly spread from the United States to Europe, facilitated by the mass movement of troops during World War I.

- **Troop Transports**: The crowded conditions on troop transports allowed the virus to spread rapidly among soldiers, who then carried it to the Western Front and beyond.
- **European Outbreaks**: By the spring of 1918, the flu had spread to major European cities, including Paris, London, and Madrid. Spain, which remained neutral during the war and had a free press, reported extensively on the outbreak, leading to the misnomer "Spanish Flu."

Global Dissemination

The Spanish Flu spread rapidly across the globe, reaching even remote regions within months.

- **Asia and Africa**: The virus spread to Asia, affecting countries such as India, China, and Japan, as well as many parts of Africa. In India, the pandemic killed an estimated 12 to 17 million people.
- **Pacific Islands**: Isolated Pacific islands, such as Samoa and Fiji, also experienced devastating outbreaks, often introduced by ships docking at their ports.
- **Americas**: In North and South America, the flu spread through cities and rural areas alike, exacerbated by public gatherings and

the movement of people seeking better living conditions.

4.1.2 Devastation and Mortality
High Mortality Rates

The Spanish Flu's mortality rate was extraordinarily high, with the pandemic killing an estimated 50 million people worldwide, though some estimates suggest the death toll could be as high as 100 million.

- **Young Adults**: Unlike typical influenza viruses that predominantly affect the very young and the elderly, the Spanish Flu had a disproportionately high mortality rate among young adults aged 20 to 40 years. This unusual pattern is thought to result from a phenomenon known as a cytokine storm, where a healthy immune system overreacts to the infection.
- **Global Impact**: The pandemic caused severe mortality across all continents, with some of the highest death rates occurring in densely populated regions with limited healthcare infrastructure.

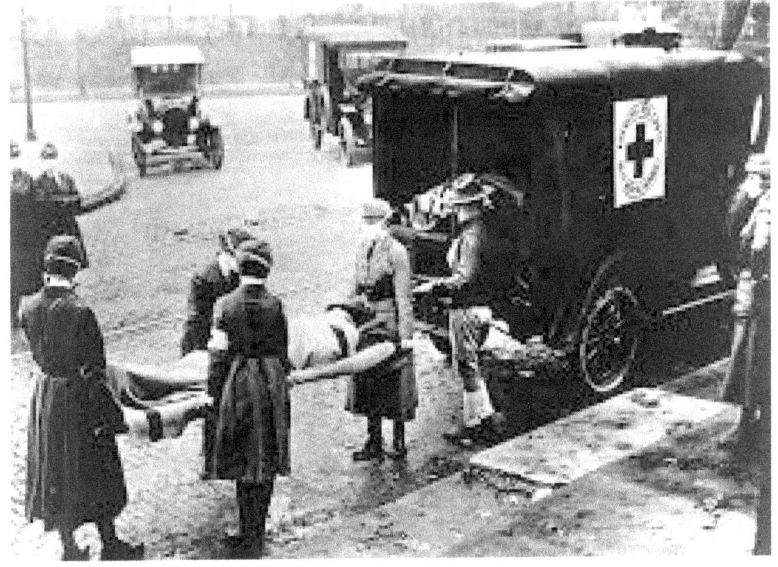

High Mortality Rate of Spanish Flu

Demographic Impact

The demographic impact of the Spanish Flu was profound, leading to significant changes in population dynamics.

- **Population Decline**: Many countries experienced sharp declines in population due to the high death toll, which also had long-term demographic effects.
- **Economic Consequences**: The loss of a significant portion of the working-age population led to economic disruptions, including labor shortages and a decrease in productivity.

Public Health Crisis

The Spanish Flu overwhelmed healthcare systems worldwide, revealing the limitations of contemporary public health infrastructure.

- **Hospital Overcrowding**: Hospitals were quickly overwhelmed by the sheer number of patients, leading to makeshift infirmaries being set up in schools, churches, and other public buildings.
- **Medical Personnel**: The shortage of medical personnel, exacerbated by the war, meant that many patients did not receive adequate care. Nurses and doctors themselves were not immune to the flu, further straining the healthcare system.

4.1.3 Spread Mechanisms

Transmission Dynamics

Understanding the mechanisms of the Spanish Flu's spread is crucial to comprehending its rapid and widespread impact.

- **Airborne Transmission**: The primary mode of transmission was through respiratory droplets expelled when infected individuals coughed or sneezed. The virus could also spread via fomites, objects or surfaces contaminated with the virus.
- **Close Contact**: Crowded living conditions, especially in military camps, urban centers, and public gatherings, facilitated the rapid spread of the virus.

Role of World War I

World War I played a significant role in the spread of the Spanish Flu, with the movement of troops and refugees acting as vectors for the virus.

- **Military Camps**: Overcrowded military camps were breeding grounds for the virus, which could spread rapidly among soldiers living in close quarters.
- **Troop Movements**: The global movement of troops facilitated the spread of the virus across continents, with infected soldiers introducing the virus to new regions.

Transportation Networks

The global transportation network of the early 20th century, including railways and ships, played a crucial role in the dissemination of the Spanish Flu.

- **Railways**: Railways enabled the virus to spread quickly within countries, reaching both urban and rural areas.
- **Maritime Travel**: Ships carried the virus across oceans, spreading it to distant lands and isolated communities.

4.2 Impact on Immigration and Travel Restrictions

4.2.1 Immigration Policies

Immigration Restrictions

In response to the Spanish Flu, many countries implemented strict immigration policies and travel restrictions to curb the spread of the virus.

- **Quarantine Measures**: Immigrants arriving from affected areas were subjected to quarantine measures, often detained for weeks before being allowed entry.
- **Travel Bans**: Some countries imposed outright travel bans on passengers from regions heavily affected by the pandemic, severely restricting international travel.

Impact on Immigrant Communities

The pandemic had a significant impact on immigrant communities, exacerbating existing social and economic challenges.

- **Economic Hardship**: Many immigrants faced economic hardship as job opportunities dwindled and public services were strained by the pandemic.
- **Social Stigma**: Immigrant communities often faced social stigma and discrimination, being unfairly blamed for the spread of the virus.

Long-Term Policy Changes

The Spanish Flu led to lasting changes in immigration policies and public health practices.

- **Health Screenings**: The pandemic underscored the importance of health screenings for immigrants, leading to more stringent health checks and quarantine procedures at borders.
- **International Cooperation**: The global nature of the pandemic highlighted the need for international cooperation in managing public health crises, paving the way for future collaborative efforts.

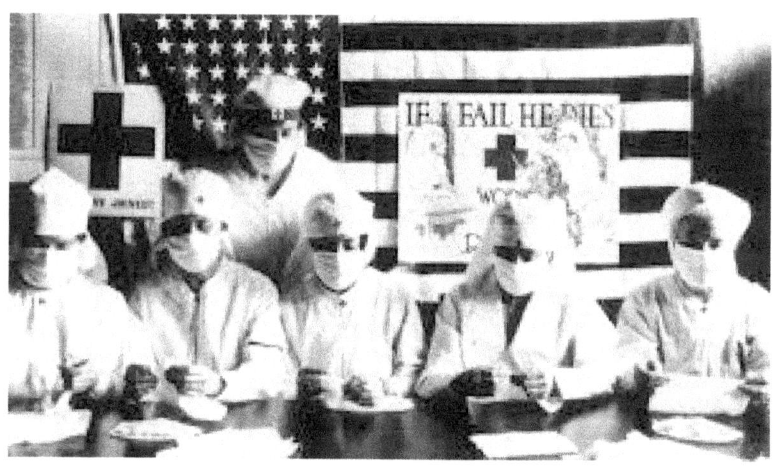

Public Health Practices in Spanish Flu

4.2.2 Travel Restrictions

National and Local Measures

Countries and local governments implemented various travel restrictions to control the spread of the Spanish Flu.

- **Public Transportation**: Restrictions were placed on public transportation, including trains and buses, to limit the movement of people and reduce transmission.

- **Curfews and Lockdowns**: Curfews and lockdowns were imposed in many cities, restricting the movement of residents and limiting public gatherings.

Impact on Commerce and Tourism

The travel restrictions had significant economic repercussions, particularly for commerce and tourism.

- **Economic Downturn**: The restrictions led to a sharp decline in economic activity, with businesses facing reduced customer traffic and supply chain disruptions.
- **Tourism Decline**: The tourism industry suffered as travel bans and health concerns kept people from traveling, leading to widespread closures of hotels, resorts, and tourist attractions.

Innovations in Public Health

The challenges posed by the Spanish Flu prompted innovations in public health and travel safety.

- **Health Protocols**: New health protocols were developed for travelers, including mandatory mask-wearing, health declarations, and enhanced sanitation measures.
- **Public Health Campaigns**: Governments launched public health campaigns to educate citizens about the virus and promote preventive measures, such as handwashing and social distancing.

The Spanish Flu's impact on early 20th-century travel and immigration underscores the profound influence of pandemics on global mobility and public health policies. By examining the origins, spread, and mortality of the Spanish Flu, along with the resultant immigration policies and travel restrictions, we gain valuable insights into the historical responses to pandemics. This understanding informs contemporary approaches to managing and mitigating the risks associated with global health crises, emphasizing the importance of preparedness, international cooperation, and public health innovation in ensuring the safety and resilience of global travel and migration systems.

CHAPTER FIVE

HIV/AIDS AND MODERN TOURISM

Introduction

The emergence of HIV/AIDS in the late 20th century marked a significant turning point in public health and had far-reaching implications for modern tourism. As a global pandemic, HIV/AIDS reshaped societal perceptions, influenced travel behavior, and necessitated new safety protocols within the tourism industry. This chapter delves into the epidemiology of HIV/AIDS, its impact on public perception, and the subsequent changes in travel patterns and safety protocols. By examining these factors, we gain insight into how a communicable disease can influence modern travel and tourism.

5.1 Epidemiology and Public Perception

5.1.1 Origins and Spread of HIV/AIDS

Origins of HIV/AIDS

HIV (Human Immunodeficiency Virus) is believed to have crossed over to humans from chimpanzees in Central Africa. The virus likely transferred through the hunting and consumption of bushmeat.

- **Early Cases:** The earliest known case of HIV dates back to the late 1950s in the Democratic Republic of Congo. Studies suggest that the virus was circulating in human populations for several decades before it was recognized as a distinct disease. The virus spread silently, unnoticed by the medical community, until it reached epidemic proportions.

- **Global Spread**: The global spread of HIV/AIDS began in the late 1970s and early 1980s. The disease was first identified among men who have sex with men in the United States, and it quickly became apparent that it was also affecting other populations, such as intravenous drug users and recipients of contaminated blood transfusions. By the mid-1980s, HIV/AIDS had been reported in multiple countries across Europe, Africa, Asia, and Latin America, highlighting its ability to cross borders and affect diverse populations.

Mechanisms of Transmission

HIV is primarily transmitted through contact with infected bodily fluids, including blood, semen, vaginal fluids, and breast milk. The primary modes of transmission include:

- **Sexual Contact**: The most common mode of transmission is through unprotected sexual intercourse with an infected partner. This can occur during vaginal, anal, or oral sex, with anal sex carrying the highest risk due to the fragile nature of the rectal lining.
- **Blood Transfusions and Needle Sharing**: HIV can be transmitted through contaminated blood transfusions, although rigorous screening processes have significantly reduced this risk. Sharing needles or syringes among intravenous drug users is another common route of transmission, as the virus can be transferred directly into the bloodstream.
- **Mother-to-Child Transmission**: An infected mother can pass the virus to her child during pregnancy, childbirth, or breastfeeding. Without intervention, the transmission rate is about 15-45%, but this can be reduced to below 5% with appropriate antiretroviral treatment and other medical interventions.

Global Epidemiology

The global epidemiology of HIV/AIDS has seen significant changes since its emergence.

- **Pandemic Scale**: By the mid-1980s, HIV/AIDS had become a global pandemic, affecting millions of people worldwide. The highest prevalence rates were recorded in sub-Saharan Africa, where the epidemic had devastating social and economic impacts, contributing to a decline in life expectancy and exacerbating poverty and inequality.
- **Prevalence and Incidence**: The prevalence and incidence of HIV/AIDS vary widely by region. Sub-Saharan Africa remains the most affected region, with countries like South Africa, Nigeria, and Mozambique having some of the highest rates of HIV infection. In contrast, regions such as Western Europe and North America have lower prevalence rates but still face challenges in controlling the epidemic. Emerging hotspots in Southeast Asia and Eastern Europe have seen rising incidence rates in recent years, often linked to high-risk behaviors such as intravenous drug use and unprotected sex.
- **Public Health Response**: The response to the HIV/AIDS pandemic has included widespread public health campaigns aimed at reducing stigma and promoting safe practices. The development of antiretroviral therapies (ART) has been a major milestone, transforming HIV from a fatal disease to a manageable chronic condition. International efforts, spearheaded by organizations like UNAIDS and the Global Fund, have focused on reducing transmission rates, improving access to treatment, and addressing the social determinants of health that contribute to the spread of the virus.

5.1.2 Public Perception and Stigma

Initial Reactions and Stigma

The initial public reaction to HIV/AIDS was characterized by fear, misunderstanding, and stigma.

- **Fear and Panic**: The early years of the HIV/AIDS epidemic were marked by widespread fear and panic. The lack of understanding about the disease and its transmission led to exaggerated fears of casual transmission through everyday contact, such as shaking hands or sharing utensils. This fear was compounded by the high mortality rate associated with AIDS in the absence of effective treatment.
- **Stigmatization**: People living with HIV/AIDS faced significant stigma and discrimination. Misconceptions about the disease led to the marginalization of affected individuals and communities, particularly those in high-risk groups such as men who have sex with men, intravenous drug users, and sex workers. This stigma not only affected the mental health and quality of life of those living with HIV/AIDS but also hindered public health efforts by discouraging people from seeking testing and treatment.

Media Influence

The media played a crucial role in shaping public perception of HIV/AIDS.

- **Sensationalism**: Media coverage often sensationalized the disease, focusing on its most dramatic and tragic aspects. Stories about celebrities dying from AIDS, such as Rock Hudson and Freddie Mercury, captured public attention but sometimes reinforced stereotypes and fears. This sensationalism contributed to the public's fear and misunderstanding of the disease.
- **Awareness Campaigns**: Over time, media coverage shifted to include more balanced and informative content. Public service announcements, documentaries, and news reports began to focus on the realities of living with HIV/AIDS, the science behind its transmission, and the importance of prevention and treatment. Campaigns featuring public figures and community leaders helped to humanize the epidemic and reduce stigma.

Cultural and Social Impact

The cultural and social impact of HIV/AIDS has been profound, influencing attitudes toward sexuality, drug use, and public health.

- **Sexual Behavior**: The epidemic prompted changes in sexual behavior, with increased emphasis on safe sex practices. Condom use became more widespread, and public health campaigns promoted regular HIV testing and sexual health education. The advent of PrEP (pre-exposure prophylaxis) has further transformed HIV prevention, offering a powerful tool for individuals at high risk of infection.
- **Public Health Policies**: The need to address HIV/AIDS led to significant changes in public health policies. Harm reduction programs, such as needle exchange initiatives, were implemented to reduce the spread of the virus among intravenous drug users. Comprehensive sex education programs were introduced in schools to provide young people with accurate information about HIV and other sexually transmitted infections. These policies have played a crucial role in reducing transmission rates and improving outcomes for people living with HIV/AIDS.

5.1.3 Advances in Treatment and Prevention

Antiretroviral Therapy (ART)

The development of antiretroviral therapy (ART) has been a major milestone in the fight against HIV/AIDS.

- **Effectiveness**: ART has proven highly effective in suppressing the virus, reducing viral load to undetectable levels, and preventing the progression to AIDS. This has transformed HIV from a death sentence into a manageable chronic condition. Patients on ART can lead long, healthy lives, significantly reducing the risk of transmission to others.
- **Accessibility**: Efforts to make ART more accessible, particularly in low- and middle-income countries, have been critical in

reducing HIV-related morbidity and mortality. Programs like the President's Emergency Plan for AIDS Relief (PEPFAR) and initiatives by the Global Fund have expanded access to ART in resource-limited settings, providing lifesaving treatment to millions of people.

Prevention Strategies

Prevention strategies have evolved to include a combination of biomedical, behavioral, and structural interventions.

- **Pre-Exposure Prophylaxis (PrEP)**: PrEP is a biomedical intervention that involves taking antiretroviral drugs to prevent HIV infection in high-risk individuals. Clinical trials have shown that PrEP can reduce the risk of HIV transmission by up to 99% when taken consistently.
- **Behavioral Interventions**: Behavioral interventions, such as promoting condom use, regular testing, and reducing the number of sexual partners, remain essential components of HIV prevention. These interventions are often tailored to the specific needs of high-risk populations, including men who have sex with men, sex workers, and intravenous drug users.
- **Structural Interventions**: Structural interventions address the social and economic factors that contribute to HIV risk. This includes efforts to reduce poverty, improve access to education and healthcare, and combat stigma and discrimination. By addressing these underlying determinants, structural interventions can create an environment that supports healthy behaviors and reduces the risk of HIV transmission.

Global Initiatives

Global initiatives have played a key role in the fight against HIV/AIDS.

- **UNAIDS**: The Joint United Nations Programme on HIV/AIDS (UNAIDS) has been instrumental in coordinating international efforts to combat the epidemic. UNAIDS sets global targets, advocates for human rights, and provides technical support to countries to develop and implement effective HIV/AIDS programs.

- **Global Fund**: The Global Fund to Fight AIDS, Tuberculosis, and Malaria provides financial support to countries to implement comprehensive HIV/AIDS programs. The Global Fund focuses on prevention, treatment, and care, and has played a crucial role in scaling up access to ART and other essential services.

5.2 Changes in Travel Patterns and Safety Protocols
5.2.1 Impact on Travel Behavior
Traveler Awareness

The emergence of HIV/AIDS has heightened awareness among travelers regarding health risks and safety measures.

- **Health Precautions**: Travelers have become more vigilant about taking health precautions. This includes avoiding risky behaviors, such as unprotected sex and sharing needles, getting vaccinated against preventable diseases, and carrying preventive medications like PrEP. Travel health clinics often provide information and resources to help travelers protect themselves against HIV and other infections.
- **Medical Tourism**: The need for specialized treatment and access to ART has led to an increase in medical tourism. Individuals from countries with limited healthcare resources often travel to destinations with advanced medical facilities to receive HIV treatment and care. This has created a niche market within the tourism industry, with some destinations actively promoting their healthcare services to attract medical tourists.

Destination Preferences

HIV/AIDS has influenced travelers' destination preferences, with some destinations perceived as higher risk than others.

- **Risk Assessment**: Travelers often assess the risk of HIV infection when choosing destinations. This assessment is particularly relevant for those engaging in activities that may increase exposure, such as sexual tourism. Countries with high HIV prevalence rates may be viewed as higher risk, leading some travelers to avoid these destinations.
- **Health Infrastructure**: The quality of health infrastructure and the availability of medical services in a destination have become important considerations for travelers. Destinations with robust healthcare systems, comprehensive HIV prevention and treatment programs, and accessible health services are often preferred by health-conscious travelers.

5.2.2 Safety Protocols and Industry Response
Travel Industry Adaptations

The travel industry has adapted to the challenges posed by HIV/AIDS, implementing safety protocols to protect travelers and staff.

- **Health Screenings**: Some travel companies and destinations have introduced health screenings for travelers, particularly those coming from regions with high HIV prevalence. These screenings aim to identify and manage potential health risks, ensuring the safety of both travelers and local populations.
- **Information Dissemination**: Travel companies provide information on HIV prevention and safe practices to travelers, often in collaboration with public health authorities. This information includes guidance on safe sex practices, the importance of regular HIV testing, and access to medical services while traveling.

Workplace Policies

The travel and tourism industry has developed workplace policies to address the impact of HIV/AIDS on employees.

- **Employee Health Programs**: Many companies offer health programs that include regular testing, access to ART, and support services for employees living with HIV. These programs aim to promote the health and well-being of employees, reduce absenteeism, and improve productivity.
- **Anti-Discrimination Policies**: To combat stigma and discrimination, companies have implemented anti-discrimination policies and training programs to foster inclusive workplaces. These policies ensure that employees living with HIV are treated fairly and have equal opportunities for career advancement.

Collaborative Efforts

Collaborative efforts between the travel industry, public health organizations, and governments have been crucial in addressing the challenges of HIV/AIDS.

- **Public-Private Partnerships**: Public-private partnerships have facilitated the implementation of comprehensive HIV prevention and treatment programs. These partnerships leverage the resources and expertise of both sectors to address the epidemic effectively, particularly in high-risk areas.
- **International Guidelines**: International guidelines, such as those developed by the World Health Organization (WHO) and the International Air Transport Association (IATA), provide a framework for managing health risks in the travel industry. These guidelines offer best practices for health screenings, information dissemination, and the implementation of safety protocols.

The HIV/AIDS pandemic has had a profound impact on modern tourism, reshaping public perception, travel behavior, and safety protocols. By examining the epidemiology of HIV/AIDS, its influence on public perception, and the resulting changes in travel patterns and industry responses, we gain valuable insights into the interplay between communicable diseases and global travel. This understanding highlights the importance of ongoing efforts to address public health challenges, promote safe travel practices, and ensure the resilience of the tourism industry in the face of future health crises.

54

CHAPTER SIX

SARS AND THE EARLY 2000S

Introduction

The outbreak of Severe Acute Respiratory Syndrome (SARS) in the early 2000s stands as a watershed moment in the intersection of global public health and the tourism industry. SARS, caused by a novel coronavirus (SARS-CoV), emerged suddenly and alarmingly, leading to widespread fear and a swift international response. This chapter explores the origins, rapid spread, containment efforts, and far-reaching impacts of SARS, particularly on Asian tourism markets. By examining these aspects, we gain insight into how a significant health crisis can disrupt global travel, affect economies, and reshape public health policies.

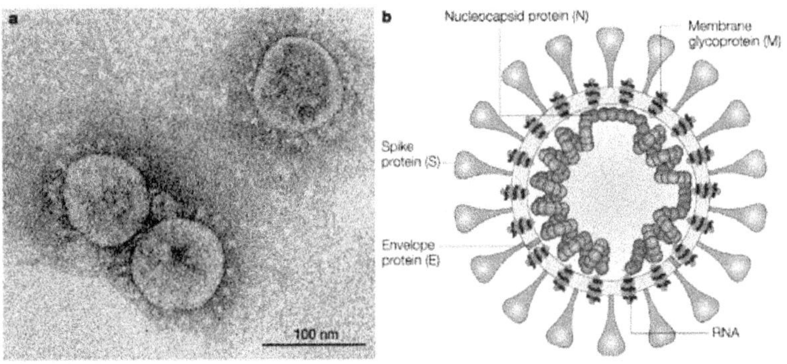

Structure of SARS-CoV

6.1 Outbreak and Containment
6.1.1 Emergence of SARS
Origin and Spread

Severe Acute Respiratory Syndrome (SARS) emerged suddenly in November 2002 in Guangdong Province, China. The virus is believed to have originated from animal markets in the region, where it jumped from animal reservoirs to humans through close contact and exposure to infected wildlife. While the exact species acting as the primary reservoir remains uncertain, early cases implicated palm civets and other mammals in the transmission chain.

- **Origins**: Initial cases of SARS were linked to the handling and consumption of wild animals in Guangdong's wet markets. The virus, a novel coronavirus, was initially misdiagnosed as atypical pneumonia, allowing it to spread unchecked. This zoonotic transmission underscored the risks associated with human interaction with wildlife and the lack of biosecurity measures in these markets.
- **Animal to Human Transmission**: The close quarters of wet markets, combined with poor sanitary conditions, facilitated the zoonotic transmission of the virus from animals to humans. Subsequent human-to-human transmission occurred primarily through respiratory droplets, which are expelled when an infected person coughs or sneezes.

By early 2003, SARS had rapidly transcended national borders, facilitated by international air travel. Infected individuals, often unknowingly carrying the virus, traveled to various countries, sparking outbreaks in densely populated urban centers like Hong Kong, Singapore, Vietnam, and even as far as Toronto, Canada. The swift and widespread transmission of the virus raised global alarm, prompting the World Health Organization (WHO) to declare SARS a global health alert, signaling its potential to cause severe public health crises.

- **Travel Transmission**: International travel played a significant role in the rapid global spread of SARS. One of the most notable early cases involved a doctor from Guangdong who traveled to Hong Kong, staying at the Metropole Hotel. Here, he infected other guests who then traveled to other countries, spreading the virus further.
- **Urban Centers**: The virus spread most rapidly in densely populated urban areas, exacerbated by high population density, frequent public transportation use, and crowded living conditions. These factors created environments where the virus could easily transmit from person to person.

Containment Efforts
Public Health Response
Governments affected by SARS responded swiftly with stringent public health measures aimed at curbing the spread of the virus. These measures included quarantine protocols, travel advisories, and health screenings, all designed to limit the movement of infected individuals and prevent further transmission.

- **Quarantine Protocols**: Infected individuals and those suspected of exposure were immediately isolated to prevent further transmission within communities and healthcare settings. Large-scale quarantines were implemented in cities with significant outbreaks. These measures, though drastic, were essential in containing the virus.
- **Travel Advisories**: Governments issued travel advisories urging against non-essential travel to affected regions, particularly in Asia where the outbreak initially took hold. These advisories aimed to reduce the movement of potentially infected individuals across borders and limit the spread of the virus.

- **Health Screenings**: Airports, seaports, and other entry points implemented rigorous health screenings. These screenings included temperature checks and health questionnaires to detect potential cases among travelers and prevent the spread of the virus across international travel routes.

Global Collaboration

The WHO played a pivotal role in coordinating international efforts to combat SARS, fostering collaboration among affected countries, healthcare systems, and research institutions.

- **Transparency**: The WHO facilitated information sharing and data transparency among affected nations. This transparency was crucial for the swift identification of new outbreaks and the implementation of targeted containment measures. Countries were encouraged to report cases promptly and accurately, helping to build a comprehensive global response.
- **Cooperation**: International cooperation was essential in developing effective treatment protocols and preventive measures. Collaboration extended to sharing research findings, medical expertise, and resources to bolster global readiness and response capabilities. Efforts included joint research initiatives, shared access to medical supplies, and coordinated public health campaigns.

The coordinated efforts to contain SARS through stringent public health measures and international collaboration highlighted the importance of proactive response strategies in mitigating future pandemics. The experience gained from managing SARS informed the development of global health protocols and preparedness plans for future outbreaks.

6.1.2 Impact on Health Systems
Healthcare Challenges
Healthcare Overload

Regions severely affected by SARS faced unprecedented challenges within their healthcare systems. The sudden surge in patients requiring intensive care strained medical resources and personnel, leading to significant disruptions in healthcare delivery.

- **Shortages**: The surge in patients requiring intensive care strained medical resources, leading to shortages of critical supplies such as personal protective equipment (PPE), ventilators, and medications needed to manage severe respiratory symptoms. Hospitals were overwhelmed, and supply chains struggled to keep up with the demand for essential medical equipment.
- **Staff Burnout**: Healthcare workers endured prolonged and intense workloads under stressful conditions. The physical and emotional toll contributed to widespread fatigue, mental health strains, and a heightened risk of burnout among medical professionals. The constant exposure to the virus also increased the risk of infection among healthcare workers, further exacerbating the strain on the healthcare system.

Adaptation and Response

Healthcare systems responded with adaptive strategies to manage the crisis effectively. These strategies aimed to optimize resources, protect healthcare workers, and ensure the continuity of care for all patients.

- **Enhanced Infection Control**: Hospitals and healthcare facilities implemented rigorous infection control protocols. These measures included strict isolation procedures for suspected and confirmed cases, enhanced disinfection practices, and training for healthcare personnel in the proper use of PPE. These protocols were critical in preventing nosocomial (hospital-acquired) infections and protecting both patients and staff.
- **Resource Reallocation**: To meet the overwhelming demand for SARS-related care, healthcare providers redirected resources

and personnel. This reallocation involved temporarily shifting focus from routine medical services to prioritize SARS treatment and containment efforts. Non-urgent procedures were postponed, and specialized SARS treatment units were established to concentrate resources and expertise.

The healthcare challenges posed by SARS underscored the importance of preparedness and flexibility in responding to emerging infectious diseases. The lessons learned from managing SARS have informed subsequent efforts to strengthen healthcare systems' resilience to future pandemics.

6.2 Impact on Asian Tourism Markets

6.2.1 Economic Fallout

Tourism Decline

The outbreak of Severe Acute Respiratory Syndrome (SARS) had a profound and immediate impact on Asian tourism markets, triggering a sharp decline in tourist arrivals and causing significant economic losses across the region.

- **Visitor Deterrence**: The issuance of travel advisories by governments around the world strongly discouraged international and domestic travel to affected areas in Asia. Travelers, fearing the risk of contracting SARS, opted to postpone or cancel their trips, leading to a sudden drop in tourist arrivals. This decline was particularly pronounced in major tourism hubs such as Hong Kong, Singapore, and Thailand.
- **Economic Losses**: Asian countries heavily reliant on tourism, such as Hong Kong, Singapore, Thailand, and Malaysia, experienced substantial declines in revenue from the hospitality, entertainment, and related industries. Hotels, restaurants, tour operators, and airlines faced reduced bookings and cancellations, exacerbating financial strain across the tourism sector. The economic impact extended beyond the immediate tourism industry, affecting related sectors such as retail and transportation.

The economic fallout from SARS highlighted the vulnerability of tourism-dependent economies to global health crises. The sudden and severe impact on tourism revenues underscored the need for robust crisis management strategies to mitigate the effects of such disruptions.

6.2.2 Recovery and Resilience

Tourism Recovery

Despite the initial setbacks caused by SARS, Asian tourism markets demonstrated resilience and gradual recovery. The recovery process involved restoring traveler confidence, implementing safety measures, and promoting diverse tourism offerings.

- **Long-term Effects**: Over time, affected countries implemented effective containment measures and communicated transparently with the public and international travelers. This proactive approach helped to restore confidence in the safety of visiting Asian destinations. Public health campaigns emphasized the successful containment of the virus and the measures in place to protect visitors.
- **Resilience Strategies**: Governments and tourism stakeholders implemented strategic initiatives to rebuild trust and revitalize the tourism industry:

  - **Promoting Safety Protocols**: To reassure travelers of their safety, stringent health and safety protocols were introduced. Measures included enhanced sanitation practices in hotels and public spaces, mandatory temperature screenings at airports, and the provision of personal protective equipment for hospitality staff. These protocols were widely publicized to highlight the commitment to visitor safety.
  - **Diversifying Offerings**: Recognizing the risks associated with overdependence on specific tourism markets, Asian countries diversified their tourism offerings. Efforts were made to promote cultural, ecological, and adventure tourism,

thereby appealing to a broader range of travelers and reducing vulnerability to future disruptions. Marketing campaigns showcased lesser-known destinations and unique experiences to attract visitors.

The recovery and resilience of the Asian tourism market after SARS serve as a testament to the sector's ability to adapt and bounce back from significant disruptions. The strategies implemented during this period have provided valuable insights for managing future crises and ensuring sustainable tourism growth.

The impact of SARS on Asian tourism markets underscores the vulnerability of the industry to global health crises. The severe economic fallout resulting from reduced tourist arrivals highlighted the need for robust crisis management strategies and resilience-building measures within the tourism sector. By adopting proactive safety measures, promoting diverse tourism offerings, and fostering international cooperation, Asian countries navigated the challenges posed by SARS and emerged with valuable lessons in mitigating risks and ensuring sustainable tourism growth in the face of future health emergencies.

The SARS outbreak of the early 2000s stands as a pivotal event in public health and tourism history. It not only revealed the fragility of global health systems but also underscored the interconnectedness of nations in the face of a pandemic. The lessons learned from SARS have informed subsequent public health responses to infectious diseases, highlighting the importance of preparedness, collaboration, and resilience. As we continue to face new health challenges, the experiences and insights gained from the SARS outbreak remain crucial in shaping our approach to safeguarding public health and sustaining global tourism.

CHAPTER SEVEN

H1N1 Influenza (Swine Flu)

Introduction

The H1N1 Influenza, commonly known as Swine Flu, emerged in 2009 and rapidly evolved into a global pandemic. This chapter examines the global response to H1N1, the travel advisories issued, and the subsequent economic impact on the tourism industry. By analyzing these elements, we gain insights into the complexities of managing a global health crisis and its repercussions on international travel and economies.

7.1 Global Response and Travel Advisories

7.1.1 Initial Outbreak and Identification

Emergence of H1N1

H1N1 influenza, a novel strain of the influenza virus, was first identified in April 2009 in Mexico. The virus contained a unique combination of influenza genes not previously identified in animals or humans, indicating a new variant with pandemic potential.

- **Initial Cases:** The first cases were detected in Veracruz, Mexico, where patients presented with typical flu-like symptoms. The rapid spread of the virus in Mexico raised concerns among public health officials due to its high transmission rate and the severity of symptoms in some cases.

- **Zoonotic Origins**: Like SARS, H1N1 was a zoonotic virus, believed to have originated in pigs before jumping to humans. The genetic makeup of the virus included elements of avian, swine, and human flu viruses, which contributed to its ability to spread rapidly among human populations.

Spread and Recognition

The virus quickly spread beyond Mexico, with cases reported in the United States, Canada, and several other countries within weeks of its identification. The World Health Organization (WHO) declared the H1N1 outbreak a public health emergency of international concern on April 25, 2009.

- **Rapid Spread**: The H1N1 virus spread globally within a short period due to its high transmissibility and the interconnected nature of international travel. By June 2009, the WHO declared H1N1 a pandemic, marking the first influenza pandemic in over 40 years.
- **Public Awareness**: Public awareness campaigns were launched to inform populations about the symptoms of H1N1, preventive measures, and the importance of seeking medical attention if infected. Governments and health organizations utilized various media channels to disseminate information and curb the spread of misinformation.

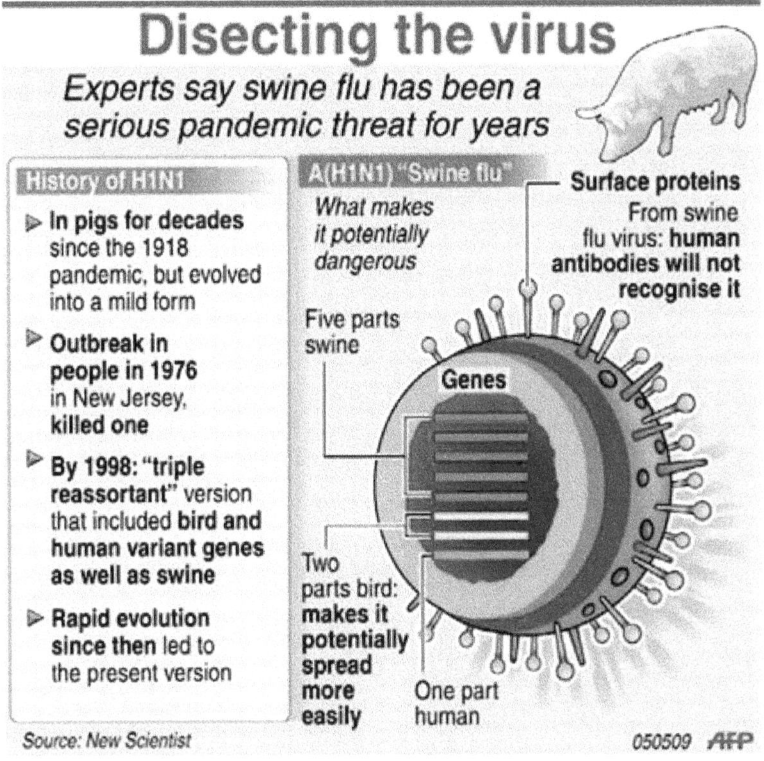

The Swine Flu Story

7.1.2 International Health Organizations' Response
World Health Organization (WHO)

The WHO played a critical role in coordinating the global response to the H1N1 pandemic. It provided guidance to countries on managing the outbreak, issued travel advisories, and facilitated the sharing of information and resources.

- **Pandemic Phases**: The WHO developed a six-phase pandemic alert system to guide countries in their response efforts. This system ranged from initial identification (Phase 1) to widespread human transmission (Phase 6), helping nations implement appropriate measures based on the severity of the outbreak.

- **Travel Advisories**: The WHO issued travel advisories recommending caution for international travel to affected regions. These advisories included guidelines on personal hygiene, the use of masks, and the importance of avoiding crowded places to reduce the risk of infection.

Centers for Disease Control and Prevention (CDC)

The CDC in the United States collaborated with the WHO and other international health bodies to monitor the spread of H1N1, provide updates, and develop response strategies.

- **Surveillance and Reporting**: The CDC established enhanced surveillance systems to track the spread of H1N1, collect data on infection rates, and monitor the effectiveness of interventions. This data was critical in informing public health policies and response measures.
- **Public Health Guidelines**: The CDC issued guidelines for healthcare providers, public health officials, and the general public on preventing and managing H1N1 infections. These guidelines included recommendations on vaccination, antiviral treatments, and non-pharmaceutical interventions such as social distancing and hand hygiene.

7.1.3 National Responses
Mexico

As the epicenter of the initial outbreak, Mexico implemented a range of measures to contain the virus and protect its population.

- **Quarantine and Isolation**: Mexican authorities quickly imposed quarantines in affected areas, isolating individuals suspected of being infected to prevent further spread. Schools, businesses, and public places were temporarily closed to reduce transmission.

- **Public Health Campaigns**: The government launched extensive public health campaigns to educate citizens about H1N1 symptoms, preventive measures, and the importance of vaccination. Public spaces were disinfected regularly, and hand sanitizers were distributed widely.

United States

The United States responded promptly to the H1N1 outbreak with coordinated efforts between federal, state, and local health agencies.

- **Vaccination Campaign**: The U.S. launched a massive vaccination campaign once an H1N1 vaccine became available. The campaign prioritized high-risk groups such as healthcare workers, pregnant women, and individuals with underlying health conditions.
- **Public Information**: The government and health agencies provided continuous updates on the status of the outbreak, preventive measures, and treatment options. Public service announcements and online resources were used to disseminate information widely.

Other Countries

Countries around the world implemented various measures based on their public health infrastructure, resources, and the severity of the outbreak.

- **Travel Restrictions**: Several countries imposed travel restrictions and entry bans for individuals coming from highly affected regions. Airports and border crossings implemented health screenings to detect and isolate infected travelers.
- **Healthcare System Preparedness**: Nations ramped up their healthcare system preparedness, increasing the availability of antiviral medications, expanding hospital capacities, and training healthcare workers to manage H1N1 cases effectively.

7.1.4 Travel Advisories and Restrictions
Impact on International Travel

The issuance of travel advisories and restrictions had a significant impact on international travel, affecting tourism, business travel, and international conferences.

- **Tourism Industry**: The tourism industry faced substantial disruptions as travelers canceled or postponed trips due to fear of contracting H1N1. Airlines, hotels, and tour operators experienced declines in bookings and revenue.
- **Business Travel**: Business travel was also affected, with companies restricting travel for employees and encouraging virtual meetings to minimize risk. International conferences and events were either canceled or postponed, further impacting the travel sector.

Health Screenings and Quarantine Measures

Countries implemented health screenings and quarantine measures at points of entry to detect and isolate infected individuals.

- **Airport Screenings**: Airports worldwide introduced health screenings, including temperature checks and health questionnaires, to identify potential H1N1 cases among travelers. These measures aimed to prevent the virus from spreading across borders.
- **Quarantine Protocols**: Quarantine protocols were established for travelers coming from high-risk areas. Infected individuals and those suspected of exposure were isolated to prevent further transmission.

Public Perception and Compliance

Public perception and compliance with travel advisories and restrictions played a crucial role in the effectiveness of these measures.

- **Compliance Rates**: Compliance rates varied depending on public trust in government and health authorities. Clear communication and transparency were essential in ripple gaining public cooperation.
- **Perception of Risk**: The perceived risk of contracting H1N1 influenced travel behavior. Public awareness campaigns emphasized the importance of following travel advisories and preventive measures to reduce the risk of infection.

7.2 Economic Impact on Tourism

7.2.1 Immediate Economic Effects

Decline in Tourism Revenues

The H1N1 pandemic had an immediate and profound impact on the global tourism industry, leading to significant declines in tourism revenues.

- **Reduced Travel**: Fear of contracting H1N1 and the issuance of travel advisories led to a sharp decline in international and domestic travel. Popular tourist destinations experienced reduced visitor numbers, resulting in substantial revenue losses for the tourism sector.
- **Hotel and Airline Industry**: Hotels and airlines were among the hardest-hit industries. Cancellations and reduced bookings led to financial losses, layoffs, and, in some cases, bankruptcy for businesses unable to withstand the prolonged downturn.

Impact on Hospitality and Related Sectors

The broader hospitality sector, including restaurants, entertainment venues, and tourist attractions, also felt the economic impact of the H1N1 pandemic.

- **Restaurant Closures**: Reduced tourism and local restrictions led to decreased patronage for restaurants, many of which faced temporary or permanent closures. The decline in dining out affected suppliers and related industries, creating a ripple effect throughout the economy.

- **Entertainment and Attractions**: Tourist attractions, theme parks, and entertainment venues experienced decreased attendance, leading to revenue losses and staff layoffs. The reduction in visitor numbers also impacted local economies that relied heavily on tourism spending.

7.2.2 Long-term Economic Effects
Recovery and Resilience of the Tourism Industry

The tourism industry demonstrated resilience in the face of the H1N1 pandemic, implementing strategies to recover and rebuild.

- **Adaptation Strategies**: Tourism businesses adapted by enhancing health and safety protocols, offering flexible booking policies, and promoting local tourism to attract visitors. These strategies helped rebuild traveler confidence and support gradual recovery.
- **Government Support**: Many governments provided financial support and stimulus packages to the tourism sector to mitigate the economic impact of H1N1. Grants, loans, and tax relief measures were introduced to help businesses weather the crisis and support recovery efforts.

Changes in Travel Behavior

The H1N1 pandemic influenced changes in travel behavior and preferences, some of which have had lasting effects on the tourism industry.

- **Increased Health Awareness**: Travelers became more health-conscious, prioritizing destinations with strong health and safety measures. This shift prompted tourism businesses to maintain high standards of cleanliness and hygiene to attract visitors.
- **Preference for Domestic Travel**: The pandemic led to a surge in domestic travel as international travel restrictions remained in

place. Travelers explored local destinations, leading to increased interest in domestic tourism and benefiting local economies.

7.2.3 Case Studies of Affected Regions

Mexico

As the initial epicenter of the H1N1 outbreak, Mexico experienced significant economic challenges but also demonstrated resilience and recovery.

- **Tourism Decline**: Mexico's tourism sector faced a sharp decline in visitor numbers, leading to revenue losses and economic strain. Popular destinations such as Cancun and Mexico City saw reduced tourist arrivals, impacting local businesses and employment.
- **Recovery Efforts**: Mexico implemented targeted marketing campaigns to revive tourism, emphasizing safety measures and promoting lesser-known destinations. Government support and collaboration with the tourism industry were crucial in the recovery process.

United States

The United States, with its extensive tourism infrastructure, faced economic repercussions but also showcased adaptability and resilience.

- **Economic Impact**: Major tourist destinations, including New York City, Las Vegas, and Orlando, experienced reduced visitor numbers and revenue losses. The hospitality industry faced challenges in maintaining operations and retaining staff.
- **Adaptation Strategies**: Tourism businesses in the U.S. adapted by introducing flexible booking policies, enhancing health and safety measures, and promoting outdoor and nature-based tourism. These efforts helped attract visitors and support gradual recovery.

Asia-Pacific Region

The Asia-Pacific region, known for its vibrant tourism markets, faced economic challenges but also demonstrated resilience and innovation.

- **Impact on Tourism Hubs**: Countries such as Japan, Thailand, and Australia experienced reduced tourist arrivals and revenue losses. The decline in international visitors affected local economies and businesses reliant on tourism.
- **Innovative Recovery**: The Asia-Pacific region embraced innovation to revive tourism, leveraging technology for virtual tours, promoting domestic travel, and diversifying tourism offerings. Government support and collaboration with the private sector were key in driving recovery efforts.

The H1N1 influenza pandemic of 2009 had far-reaching impacts on global public health and the tourism industry. The rapid spread of the virus and the subsequent global response highlighted the interconnectedness of nations and the importance of coordinated efforts in managing health crises. The economic impact on the tourism industry was significant, but the resilience and adaptability demonstrated by tourism businesses and governments provided valuable lessons for future pandemics.

By examining the global response, travel advisories, and economic impact of H1N1, this chapter underscores the importance of preparedness, communication, and collaboration in mitigating the effects of infectious diseases on public health and economies. The experiences and insights gained from the H1N1 pandemic continue to inform strategies for managing health crises and sustaining the tourism industry in an increasingly interconnected world.

CHAPTER EIGHT

THE EBOLA OUTBREAK

Introduction

The Ebola virus outbreak, particularly the 2014–2016 West African epidemic, stands as one of the most severe public health crises in recent history. The virus's devastating impact on affected communities, combined with intense media coverage, reshaped global perceptions of African health systems and tourism. This chapter delves into the regional impact of the Ebola outbreak, the media's role in shaping public perception, and the resulting effects on African tourism.

8.1 Regional Impact and Media Coverage

8.1.1 Initial Outbreak and Spread

Emergence of Ebola

The Ebola virus was first identified in 1976 near the Ebola River in what is now the Democratic Republic of the Congo. The 2014–2016 outbreak, however, was the largest and most complex Ebola epidemic since the virus's discovery.

- **Initial Cases:** The outbreak began in a rural area of southeastern Guinea in December 2013, quickly spreading to urban areas and across borders into Liberia and Sierra Leone. The initial symptoms of Ebola—fever, muscle pain, and fatigue—were similar to many other diseases, leading to delays in diagnosis and containment.

- **Transmission**: Ebola spreads through direct contact with bodily fluids of infected individuals, including blood, sweat, and saliva. The high transmission rate, especially in areas with inadequate healthcare infrastructure, facilitated its rapid spread.

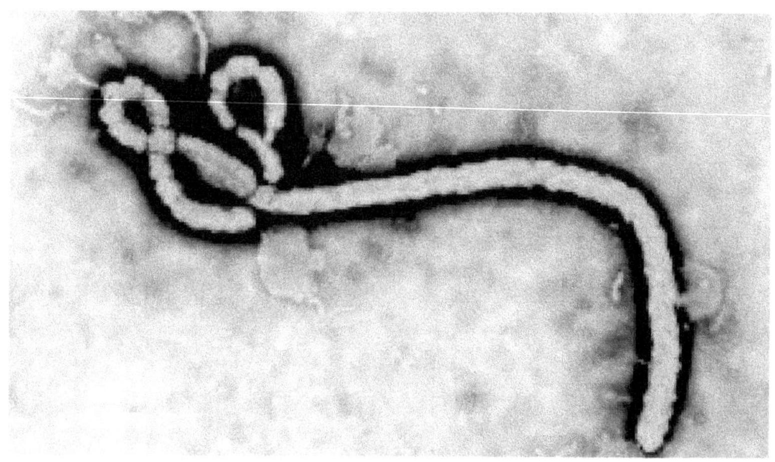

Ebola Virus

Spread Across West Africa

By mid-2014, the virus had spread to several West African countries, overwhelming healthcare systems and causing widespread fear and panic.

- **Affected Countries**: Guinea, Liberia, and Sierra Leone were the hardest hit, with thousands of confirmed cases and deaths. The epidemic also spread to Nigeria and Mali, though these countries managed to contain it more effectively.
- **Challenges**: The outbreak exposed significant gaps in healthcare infrastructure, including shortages of medical supplies, insufficient healthcare personnel, and inadequate facilities for isolating patients. Cultural practices, such as traditional burial

rites, further complicated containment efforts.

8.1.2 International Response
World Health Organization (WHO) Involvement
The WHO played a crucial role in coordinating the international response to the Ebola outbreak, despite facing criticism for its delayed reaction.

- **Declaration of Public Health Emergency**: In August 2014, the WHO declared the outbreak a Public Health Emergency of International Concern (PHEIC), prompting a more coordinated global response.
- **Response Strategies**: The WHO developed comprehensive response strategies, including infection prevention and control measures, surveillance and contact tracing, and community engagement. It also facilitated international support and resource mobilization to affected regions.

Non-Governmental Organizations (NGOs)
Numerous NGOs were instrumental in the Ebola response, providing medical care, supplies, and support to affected communities.

- **Doctors Without Borders (MSF)**: MSF was among the first organizations to respond to the outbreak, setting up treatment centers and providing critical care. Their early efforts highlighted the severity of the crisis and the urgent need for international assistance.
- **Red Cross**: The Red Cross played a significant role in community engagement and education, promoting safe practices to reduce transmission. They also assisted with safe and dignified burials, addressing cultural sensitivities while preventing further spread.

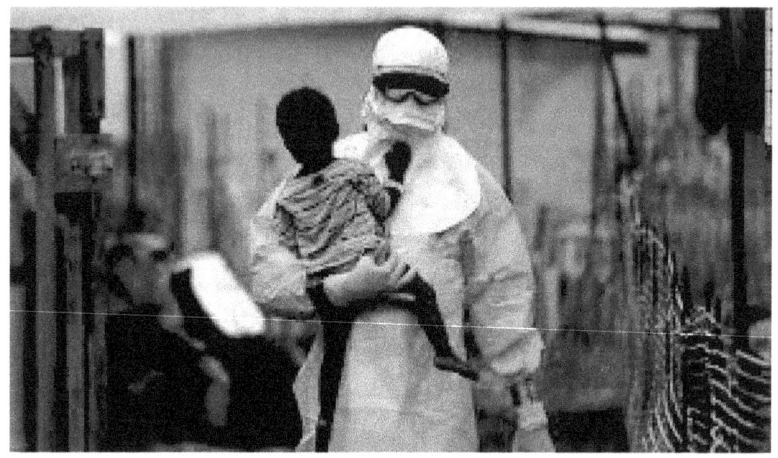

Role of NGOs in Ebola Vires Pandemic

Governmental Aid and Military Involvement

Several governments, particularly from Western countries, provided substantial aid and military support to combat the outbreak.

- **United States**: The U.S. government, through the Centers for Disease Control and Prevention (CDC) and the U.S. Agency for International Development (USAID), contributed significant resources and personnel. The U.S. military also established treatment facilities and provided logistical support.
- **United Kingdom**: The UK government focused its efforts on Sierra Leone, providing medical teams, treatment centers, and financial aid. The British military played a crucial role in constructing healthcare facilities and supporting local response efforts.

8.1.3 Media Coverage and Public Perception
Role of the Media

Media coverage of the Ebola outbreak was extensive and played a critical role in shaping public perception and response.

- **International Attention**: Major news outlets worldwide covered the outbreak extensively, highlighting the severity of the epidemic and the struggles faced by affected communities. Graphic images and stories of suffering raised global awareness and prompted calls for action.
- **Sensationalism**: While media coverage was essential in raising awareness, it also led to sensationalism and fear-mongering. Some reports exaggerated the risks of Ebola spreading globally, causing unnecessary panic and stigmatization of affected regions.

Impact on Public Perception

The intense media coverage influenced public perception and behavior both in and outside the affected regions.

- **Fear and Stigma**: Fear of Ebola led to stigma and discrimination against individuals from affected countries, even in regions far removed from the outbreak. This stigma extended to travelers, healthcare workers, and entire communities, exacerbating social and economic challenges.
- **Behavioral Changes**: Public fear influenced behavior, leading to increased demand for personal protective equipment (PPE), changes in travel patterns, and heightened vigilance in personal hygiene and health practices.

8.1.4 Social and Economic Impact

Healthcare System Overload

The Ebola outbreak placed immense pressure on already fragile healthcare systems in West Africa.

- **Resource Strain**: Hospitals and clinics were overwhelmed by the influx of Ebola patients, leading to shortages of beds, medical supplies, and healthcare workers. Many healthcare facilities were forced to shut down or limit services for non-Ebola-related health issues.

- **Healthcare Worker Impact**: Healthcare workers faced significant risks, with many contracting the virus due to inadequate PPE and infection control measures. The loss of healthcare workers further strained the system and hindered response efforts.

Economic Disruption

The economic impact of the Ebola outbreak was profound, affecting various sectors and exacerbating poverty and instability.

- **Agriculture**: Quarantine measures and movement restrictions disrupted agricultural activities, leading to food shortages and increased prices. Farmers were unable to tend to their crops, and markets were closed, affecting food security.
- **Trade and Commerce**: Trade and commerce were severely impacted as borders were closed, and international trade declined. Businesses faced losses, and unemployment rates increased, contributing to economic hardship.

8.2 Effects on African Tourism
8.2.1 Immediate Impact on Tourism
Travel Bans and Restrictions

The Ebola outbreak led to widespread travel bans and restrictions, significantly impacting tourism in affected and neighboring countries.

- **Flight Cancellations**: Many airlines suspended flights to and from affected countries, disrupting travel and tourism. This led to a sharp decline in tourist arrivals and revenue losses for the aviation industry.
- **Border Closures**: Countries implemented strict border controls and entry bans for travelers from Ebola-affected regions. These

measures, while necessary for public health, further isolated affected countries and hindered tourism.

Decline in Tourist Arrivals

The fear of Ebola and travel restrictions led to a significant decline in tourist arrivals across Africa.

- **Perception of Risk**: The perception of Africa as a high-risk destination for Ebola deterred tourists, even from countries not directly affected by the outbreak. Potential travelers canceled or postponed their plans, leading to reduced bookings for hotels, tours, and other tourism services.
- **Economic Losses**: The tourism industry, a vital economic sector for many African countries, faced substantial revenue losses. Hotels, resorts, travel agencies, and local businesses reliant on tourism income experienced financial strain and layoffs.

8.2.2 Long-term Impact on Tourism
Recovery Efforts

Efforts to revive tourism in Africa post-Ebola involved coordinated strategies and significant investment.

- **Marketing Campaigns**: Countries launched marketing campaigns to restore confidence in African destinations. These campaigns emphasized the safety of travel, highlighting unaffected regions and the beauty and diversity of African tourism offerings.
- **International Support**: International organizations and governments provided financial and technical support to help rebuild the tourism sector. This included funding for infrastructure development, training for tourism workers, and promotional activities to attract tourists.

Changes in Travel Patterns

The Ebola outbreak influenced long-term changes in travel patterns and preferences among tourists.

- **Increased Health and Safety Concerns**: Travelers became more conscious of health and safety standards, preferring destinations with robust healthcare infrastructure and crisis management capabilities. This shift prompted improvements in health and safety protocols in the tourism industry.
- **Rise of Ecotourism**: The outbreak accelerated interest in ecotourism and sustainable travel. Tourists increasingly sought out nature-based experiences and destinations that promoted environmental conservation and minimized health risks.

8.2.3 Case Studies of Affected Regions
West Africa

The countries most affected by Ebola—Guinea, Liberia, and Sierra Leone—faced significant challenges but also demonstrated resilience in rebuilding their tourism sectors.

- **Impact on Tourism**: The Ebola outbreak led to a near-total collapse of tourism in these countries. International arrivals plummeted, and tourism revenue losses were substantial. The stigma associated with Ebola further hindered recovery efforts.
- **Rebuilding Strategies**: Rebuilding efforts focused on improving healthcare infrastructure, enhancing health and safety standards, and promoting the unique cultural and natural attractions of the region. International partnerships and aid were critical in supporting these efforts.

East Africa

East African countries, though not directly affected by the outbreak, experienced indirect impacts due to the broader perception of Africa as a high-risk destination.

- **Tourism Decline**: Popular tourist destinations such as Kenya, Tanzania, and Uganda saw declines in international arrivals and bookings. The fear of Ebola, combined with travel restrictions, affected tourist confidence and travel plans.
- **Recovery Measures**: East African countries implemented measures to reassure tourists, including stringent health screenings, enhanced hygiene protocols, and targeted marketing campaigns. Efforts to diversify tourism offerings and promote domestic travel also contributed to recovery.

Southern Africa

Southern African countries experienced varying degrees of impact, with some regions facing significant challenges while others managed to sustain tourism.

- **Economic Impact**: Countries such as South Africa, Namibia, and Botswana experienced declines in tourist arrivals, particularly from international markets. The economic impact was felt across the tourism value chain, affecting accommodation, transportation, and local businesses.
- **Adaptive Strategies**: Southern African countries adapted by promoting regional travel and encouraging intra-African tourism. Marketing campaigns highlighted the safety and appeal of Southern African destinations, focusing on wildlife safaris, cultural experiences, and luxury travel.

The Ebola outbreak had profound and far-reaching impacts on public health, economies, and the tourism industry in Africa. The initial regional impact and intense media coverage shaped global perceptions and influenced travel behavior, leading to significant challenges for the tourism sector. However, the resilience and adaptability demonstrated by African countries in response to the outbreak provided valuable lessons in crisis management and recovery.

By examining the regional impact, media coverage, and effects on African tourism, this chapter highlights the importance of preparedness, communication, and collaboration in managing health crises. The experiences of the Ebola outbreak underscore the need for robust healthcare systems, effective crisis communication, and innovative strategies to sustain tourism in the face of future challenges. The lessons learned continue to inform global public health and tourism practices, ensuring that Africa remains a vibrant and attractive destination for travelers worldwide.

CHAPTER NINE

THE COVID-19 PANDEMIC

9.1 Chronology and Spread

9.1.1 Emergence of the Virus

The COVID-19 pandemic began with a cluster of pneumonia cases of unknown origin reported in Wuhan, China, in December 2019. Chinese authorities identified a novel coronavirus, later named SARS-CoV-2. The disease it caused was named COVID-19. Early cases were linked to the Huanan Seafood Wholesale Market, suggesting zoonotic transmission from animals to humans. Rapid human-to-human transmission was soon confirmed, causing the virus to spread within Wuhan and to other parts of China.

9.1.2 Global Spread

In January 2020, the World Health Organization (WHO) declared the outbreak a Public Health Emergency of International Concern. Despite aggressive containment efforts in China, the virus spread globally. By February, cases appeared in countries across Asia, Europe, and North America. In March 2020, the WHO declared COVID-19 a pandemic. Major outbreaks occurred in Italy, Spain, and the United States, overwhelming healthcare systems and prompting widespread lockdowns. By mid-2020, the virus had reached nearly every country, with significant outbreaks in Brazil,

India, and Russia, highlighting the interconnected nature of global travel and commerce.

Impact of COVID-19 on Tourism

9.1.3 Key Waves and Variants

The pandemic unfolded in multiple waves, driven by factors such as seasonality, public health measures, and virus mutations:

- **First Wave (Spring 2020):** Characterized by rapid spread and severe lockdowns. Countries like Italy, Spain, and the United States were heavily impacted.
- **Second Wave (Late 2020):** Resurgence of cases as restrictions eased and colder weather arrived. This wave saw higher peaks in many regions, including Europe and North America.
- **Subsequent Waves (2021 and beyond):** Driven by new variants with increased transmissibility and potential immune escape. Key variants included:

  ○ **Alpha (B.1.1.7):** Identified in the UK, more transmissible.

- ◦ **Beta (B.1.351):** Identified in South Africa, with partial resistance to vaccines.
- ◦ **Gamma (P.1):** Identified in Brazil, with increased transmissibility.
- ◦ **Delta (B.1.617.2):** Identified in India, significantly more transmissible and severe.
- ◦ **Omicron (B.1.1.529):** Identified in South Africa, with numerous mutations affecting transmissibility and vaccine effectiveness.

9.1.4 Vaccine Development and Distribution

The response to the pandemic saw unprecedented efforts in vaccine development:

- **Early Development:** Pharmaceutical companies like Pfizer-BioNTech, Moderna, AstraZeneca, and Johnson & Johnson rapidly developed vaccines using different technologies (mRNA, viral vector).
- **Clinical Trials:** Accelerated clinical trials demonstrated the safety and efficacy of these vaccines. By December 2020, the first vaccines received emergency use authorization.
- **Global Rollout:** Distribution began in high-income countries, leading to significant disparities in vaccination rates. Challenges included production bottlenecks, cold chain logistics for mRNA vaccines, and vaccine hesitancy.
- **Booster Shots:** As evidence of waning immunity and new variants emerged, booster doses were recommended to enhance protection, particularly for vulnerable populations.

9.2 Immediate and Long-term Effects on Global Tourism

9.2.1 Immediate Impact

The tourism industry experienced an abrupt and severe downturn:

- **Travel Bans and Quarantines:** Countries implemented strict travel bans, mandatory quarantines, and border closures to limit the spread. International travel plummeted, and tourism virtually came to a halt.
- **Industry Shutdowns:** Hotels, airlines, cruise lines, and tourist attractions faced closures. Major events, conferences, and sporting events were canceled or postponed.
- **Economic Losses:** The World Travel & Tourism Council (WTTC) estimated a loss of $4.5 trillion in 2020, with over 62 million jobs lost worldwide. Small and medium-sized enterprises (SMEs) in the tourism sector were particularly hard hit.

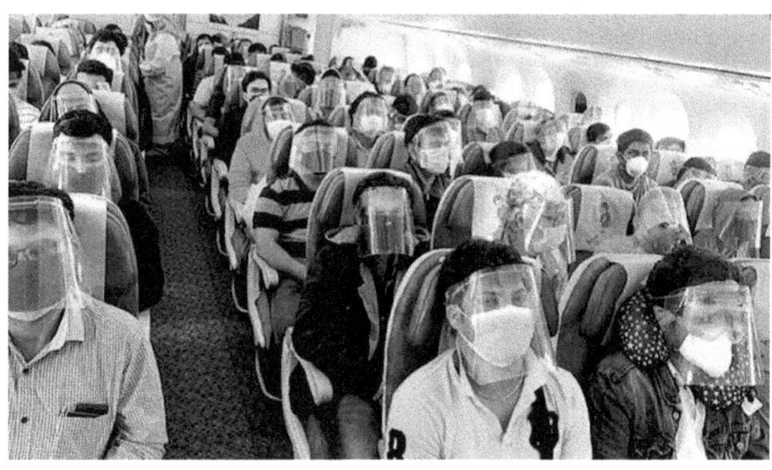

Effect of COVID-19 on Health

9.2.2 Long-term Effects

The pandemic induced lasting changes and adaptations in the tourism industry:

- **Permanent Changes:** Enhanced health protocols, such as sanitation, social distancing, and digital health passports, became standard. Travelers expected rigorous hygiene practices and flexible cancellation policies.
- **Shifts in Traveler Behavior:** There was a marked increase in domestic travel as international options remained limited. Health-conscious choices, such as opting for private accommodations and avoiding crowded places, became prevalent.
- **Economic Recovery:** Recovery was uneven, with regions and sectors dependent on international tourism facing prolonged challenges. Domestic tourism and short-haul travel recovered faster than long-haul and international tourism.

9.3 Travel Bubbles and Corridors

9.3.1 Concept and Implementation

Travel bubbles and corridors emerged as innovative solutions to mitigate the impact of travel restrictions:

- **Definition:** These agreements allowed quarantine-free travel between participating countries or regions with similar epidemiological situations.
- **Examples:**

  - **Australia-New Zealand Bubble:** One of the first successful implementations, allowing residents to travel between the two countries without quarantine.
  - **Singapore-Hong Kong Corridor:** Planned as a model for reopening travel, but faced delays and eventual cancellation due to resurgence of cases in both cities.

9.3.2 Benefits and Challenges

Travel bubbles and corridors offered both advantages and obstacles:

- **Benefits:**

  - **Economic Boost:** They provided a critical lifeline to tourism-dependent economies by reviving travel and tourism sectors.
  - **Psychological Relief:** These agreements improved morale and confidence among travelers and the general public.

- **Challenges:**

  - **Implementation Issues:** Variability in health protocols, testing standards, and readiness of healthcare systems created hurdles.
  - **Susceptibility to Resurgence:** Travel bubbles were vulnerable to collapse with new outbreaks or emergence of variants, necessitating constant monitoring and adjustments.

9.3.3 Effectiveness and Future Prospects

- **Short-term Successes:** Some regions experienced limited success, highlighting the importance of robust health protocols and cooperation between countries.
- **Long-term Viability:** While travel bubbles provided a temporary solution, their long-term viability depends on the global control of the pandemic and the establishment of standardized health measures.

9.4 Remote Work and Digital Nomads

9.4.1 Rise of Remote Work
The pandemic accelerated the adoption of remote work:

- **Initial Shift:** As offices closed during lockdowns, companies quickly transitioned to remote work to maintain operations.
- **Technological Adoption:** The use of digital tools and platforms, such as Zoom, Microsoft Teams, and Slack, surged, facilitating remote collaboration and communication.

9.4.2 Growth of Digital Nomadism

The concept of digital nomadism gained popularity:

- **Definition:** Digital nomads are remote workers who leverage technology to work from various locations around the world.
- **Popular Destinations:** Countries adapted policies to attract digital nomads, offering special visas and incentives. Notable examples include Estonia's Digital Nomad Visa, Barbados's Welcome Stamp, and Croatia's Digital Nomad Visa.

9.4.3 Economic and Social Impacts

The rise of digital nomadism had significant impacts:

- **Local Economies:** Digital nomads contributed to local economies through long-term stays and spending on accommodation, food, and services.
- **Cultural Exchange:** The influx of digital nomads fostered increased cultural exchange and diversity, benefiting both the nomads and host communities.

9.4.4 Challenges and Considerations

Digital nomadism also posed challenges:

- **Visa and Taxation Issues:** Navigating visa requirements and tax regulations across different countries was complex and often ambiguous.
- **Work-Life Balance:** Maintaining productivity while balancing the travel lifestyle required discipline and effective time management.

9.5 Case Studies: Countries and Sectors Most Affected

9.5.1 Countries

Several countries experienced severe impacts on their tourism industries:

- **Italy:** As an early epicenter in Europe, Italy saw dramatic declines in tourism, particularly in regions like Lombardy and Veneto. The lockdown measures severely impacted the hospitality sector, with many businesses closing permanently.
- **United States:** The diverse tourism landscape in the U.S. faced wide-ranging effects. Major cities like New York and Las Vegas, which rely heavily on tourism, experienced significant declines in visitor numbers and revenue.
- **Thailand:** Known for its tourism-dependent economy, Thailand faced substantial economic losses. The government introduced measures to stimulate domestic tourism and prepare for international travelers with enhanced health protocols.

9.5.2 Sectors

Key sectors within the tourism industry were particularly affected:

- **Aviation:** Airlines grounded fleets, faced financial bailouts, and implemented new health measures, such as mandatory face masks, enhanced cleaning protocols, and reduced in-flight services. Long-term changes included the adoption of digital health passports and contactless travel processes.
- **Hospitality:** Hotels and resorts closed or repurposed facilities for quarantine use. The sector adopted rigorous hygiene standards and flexible booking policies to rebuild traveler confidence.

- **Cruise Industry:** The cruise industry came to a complete halt, with numerous high-profile outbreaks on ships. Upon resumption, stringent health measures, including testing, reduced capacity, and modified itineraries, were implemented to ensure passenger safety.

Digital Nomad becomes the New Buzz word

The COVID-19 pandemic had an unparalleled impact on global tourism, reshaping the industry in both immediate and lasting ways. The implementation of travel bubbles and corridors, the rise of remote work and digital nomadism, and the severe effects on countries and key sectors illustrate the multifaceted challenges and adaptations faced by the industry. Moving forward, the tourism sector must build resilience, embrace innovation, and prepare for future health crises to ensure sustainable and safe travel experiences.

CHAPTER TEN

ECONOMIC CONSEQUENCES OF TRAVEL DISRUPTIONS

10.1 Loss of Revenue and Jobs

10.1.1 Global Impact

The COVID-19 pandemic resulted in unprecedented travel disruptions, causing significant economic losses in the global tourism industry:

- **Revenue Losses:** The World Travel & Tourism Council (WTTC) estimated a loss of $4.5 trillion in global GDP attributed to the travel and tourism sector in 2020. The industry's contribution to global GDP dropped by nearly 50%.
- **Job Losses:** Over 62 million jobs were lost worldwide in the travel and tourism sector in 2020. This represents a 18.5% decline in employment compared to the previous year, affecting millions of workers, from airline staff and hotel employees to tour guides and cruise ship workers.

- **Business Closures:** Numerous businesses within the tourism industry, particularly small and medium-sized enterprises (SMEs), faced closures due to the drastic drop in tourist activity. These closures had a ripple effect on local economies and communities reliant on tourism.

10.1.2 Regional Disparities

The economic impact of travel disruptions varied significantly across regions:

- **Europe:** Countries like Italy, Spain, and France, heavily reliant on tourism, experienced severe economic downturns. Southern European countries were particularly hard hit due to their dependency on seasonal tourism.
- **Asia-Pacific:** Countries such as Thailand, Indonesia, and the Maldives, with substantial portions of their GDP derived from tourism, faced deep economic contractions. The prolonged absence of international tourists led to widespread economic distress.
- **Americas:** The United States saw significant job losses in the tourism sector, particularly in states like Florida, Nevada, and Hawaii. Latin American countries such as Mexico and the Caribbean islands also suffered due to their dependency on international tourism.

10.2 Sector-Specific Analysis

10.2.1 Aviation

The aviation sector was among the hardest hit by the pandemic:

- **Passenger Traffic Decline:** Global passenger traffic fell by over 60% in 2020 compared to 2019, according to the International Air Transport Association (IATA). Airlines faced a severe liquidity crisis, leading to furloughs, layoffs, and in some cases, bankruptcies.

- **Financial Losses:** Airlines collectively lost an estimated $370 billion in passenger revenue in 2020. Major airlines, including Lufthansa, American Airlines, and Delta Air Lines, reported substantial financial losses and sought government bailouts to stay afloat.

- **Adaptations and Recovery:** Airlines implemented strict health and safety measures, including mandatory face masks, enhanced cleaning protocols, and contactless check-in processes. The sector gradually recovered with the rollout of vaccines and the lifting of travel restrictions, but challenges such as fluctuating travel demand and new variants persisted.

Economic Brakdown in Aviation Industry

10.2.2 Hospitality

The hospitality sector faced severe disruptions due to travel bans and lockdowns:

- **Occupancy Rates:** Hotels worldwide saw occupancy rates plummet to historic lows. In major tourist cities, occupancy rates dropped below 20% at the height of the pandemic.
- **Revenue Per Available Room (RevPAR):** RevPAR, a key performance metric for hotels, saw significant declines. In Europe and North America, RevPAR fell by over 50% in 2020 compared to the previous year.
- **Business Adaptations:** Many hotels repurposed their facilities to serve as quarantine centers or accommodations for essential workers. The sector focused on implementing rigorous hygiene standards and flexible booking policies to attract and reassure guests as travel gradually resumed.

10.2.3 Cruises

The cruise industry came to a complete halt due to the pandemic:

- **Suspension of Operations:** Major cruise lines suspended operations globally, leading to massive financial losses and widespread layoffs. High-profile outbreaks on ships, such as the Diamond Princess, severely damaged the industry's reputation.
- **Economic Impact:** The cruise industry contributed significantly to the economies of port cities and coastal regions. The suspension of cruises resulted in substantial economic losses for these communities.
- **Health and Safety Measures:** Upon resumption of operations, cruise lines implemented stringent health protocols, including mandatory testing, reduced passenger capacity, and modified itineraries. These measures aimed to rebuild consumer confidence and ensure the safety of passengers and crew.

10.3 Government Stimulus Packages

10.3.1 Types of Support

Governments worldwide introduced various stimulus packages and support measures to mitigate the economic impact on the tourism industry:

- **Financial Aid:** Direct financial assistance to businesses, including grants, loans, and subsidies, helped maintain liquidity and prevent bankruptcies. Examples include the Paycheck Protection Program (PPP) in the United States and furlough schemes in the United Kingdom.
- **Tax Relief:** Tax deferrals, reductions, and exemptions provided immediate financial relief to tourism-related businesses. This included deferred VAT payments, reduced corporate tax rates, and exemption from tourism-specific taxes.
- **Operational Support:** Measures to support operational continuity included subsidies for employee wages, rent relief, and utility cost reductions. Governments also facilitated access to credit and reduced regulatory burdens to help businesses survive the crisis.

10.3.2 Effectiveness and Challenges

- **Short-term Relief:** Government support measures provided essential short-term relief, preventing widespread bankruptcies and maintaining employment levels in the tourism sector.
- **Long-term Recovery:** The effectiveness of these measures in driving long-term recovery varied. Some countries faced challenges in efficiently distributing aid, while others struggled with the fiscal burden of prolonged support.
- **Innovation and Adaptation:** Governments encouraged innovation and adaptation within the tourism sector, promoting digital transformation, sustainable practices, and new business models to enhance resilience and competitiveness.

10.4 Case Studies of Tourism-Dependent Economies

10.4.1 Thailand

Thailand's economy heavily relies on tourism, accounting for approximately 20% of its GDP:

- **Economic Impact:** The pandemic led to a sharp contraction in Thailand's GDP, with the tourism sector bearing the brunt of the impact. The loss of international tourists caused widespread economic distress, particularly in popular tourist destinations like Bangkok, Phuket, and Chiang Mai.
- **Government Response:** The Thai government introduced a series of measures to support the tourism industry, including financial aid packages, tax relief, and domestic tourism promotion campaigns. Initiatives like the "We Travel Together" program aimed to stimulate domestic travel and support local businesses.
- **Recovery Efforts:** Thailand focused on preparing for the return of international tourists with enhanced health protocols and marketing campaigns promoting the country as a safe destination. The introduction of special tourist visas and the development of travel bubbles were part of these efforts.

10.4.2 Greece

Greece, with tourism contributing around 25% of its GDP, faced severe economic challenges:

- **Economic Impact:** The pandemic caused a significant decline in tourist arrivals, leading to substantial revenue losses and increased unemployment in the tourism sector. Popular destinations such as Athens, Santorini, and Mykonos saw dramatic drops in visitor numbers.
- **Government Response:** The Greek government implemented a comprehensive support package, including financial aid, tax

relief, and subsidies for businesses and workers in the tourism sector. Efforts to promote domestic tourism and extend the tourist season were also undertaken.

- **Recovery Efforts:** Greece launched marketing campaigns highlighting the country's safety and attractiveness as a tourist destination. The government collaborated with the private sector to implement health and safety protocols, ensuring a safe environment for visitors.

10.4.3 Maldives

The Maldives, with tourism accounting for over 30% of its GDP, experienced profound economic impacts:

- **Economic Impact:** The complete halt of international travel led to a severe economic downturn. The tourism-dependent economy faced significant revenue losses, and many resorts and businesses closed temporarily or permanently.
- **Government Response:** The Maldivian government introduced a range of measures to support the tourism industry, including financial aid, tax relief, and targeted support for SMEs. Efforts to promote domestic tourism and attract international tourists through marketing campaigns were intensified.
- **Recovery Efforts:** The Maldives implemented strict health protocols and promoted the country as a safe and exclusive destination. The government introduced special visa programs and incentives to attract long-stay tourists and remote workers.

10.5 Summary and Conclusions

The economic consequences of travel disruptions due to the COVID-19 pandemic were profound and far-reaching, affecting revenue, employment, and business operations across the tourism industry. Different sectors, such as aviation, hospitality, and cruises, faced unique challenges and adapted in various ways to survive the crisis. Government stimulus packages provided crucial support, but the long-term recovery required innovation, adaptation, and resilience. Case studies of tourism-dependent economies like Thailand, Greece, and the Maldives highlight the severe impacts and the efforts undertaken to revive and sustain the tourism sector. Moving forward, the industry must continue to build resilience, embrace innovation, and prepare for future disruptions to ensure sustainable growth and recovery.

CHAPTER ELEVEN

SOCIAL AND CULTURAL IMPACTS

10.1 Loss of Revenue and Jobs

10.1.1 Global Impact

The COVID-19 pandemic resulted in unprecedented travel disruptions, causing significant economic losses in the global tourism industry:

- **Revenue Losses:** The World Travel & Tourism Council (WTTC) estimated a loss of $4.5 trillion in global GDP attributed to the travel and tourism sector in 2020. The industry's contribution to global GDP dropped by nearly 50%.
- **Job Losses:** Over 62 million jobs were lost worldwide in the travel and tourism sector in 2020. This represents a 18.5% decline in employment compared to the previous year, affecting millions of workers, from airline staff and hotel employees to tour guides and cruise ship workers.
- **Business Closures:** Numerous businesses within the tourism industry, particularly small and medium-sized enterprises (SMEs), faced closures due to the drastic drop in tourist activity. These closures had a ripple effect on local economies and communities reliant on tourism.

10.1.2 Regional Disparities

The economic impact of travel disruptions varied significantly across regions:

- **Europe:** Countries like Italy, Spain, and France, heavily reliant on tourism, experienced severe economic downturns. Southern European countries were particularly hard hit due to their dependency on seasonal tourism.
- **Asia-Pacific:** Countries such as Thailand, Indonesia, and the Maldives, with substantial portions of their GDP derived from tourism, faced deep economic contractions. The prolonged absence of international tourists led to widespread economic distress.
- **Americas:** The United States saw significant job losses in the tourism sector, particularly in states like Florida, Nevada, and Hawaii. Latin American countries such as Mexico and the Caribbean islands also suffered due to their dependency on international tourism.

10.2 Sector-Specific Analysis

10.2.1 Aviation

The aviation sector was among the hardest hit by the pandemic:

- **Passenger Traffic Decline:** Global passenger traffic fell by over 60% in 2020 compared to 2019, according to the International Air Transport Association (IATA). Airlines faced a severe liquidity crisis, leading to furloughs, layoffs, and in some cases, bankruptcies.
- **Financial Losses:** Airlines collectively lost an estimated $370 billion in passenger revenue in 2020. Major airlines, including Lufthansa, American Airlines, and Delta Air Lines, reported substantial financial losses and sought government bailouts to stay afloat.

- **Adaptations and Recovery:** Airlines implemented strict health and safety measures, including mandatory face masks, enhanced cleaning protocols, and contactless check-in processes. The sector gradually recovered with the rollout of vaccines and the lifting of travel restrictions, but challenges such as fluctuating travel demand and new variants persisted.

10.2.2 Hospitality

The hospitality sector faced severe disruptions due to travel bans and lockdowns:

- **Occupancy Rates:** Hotels worldwide saw occupancy rates plummet to historic lows. In major tourist cities, occupancy rates dropped below 20% at the height of the pandemic.
- **Revenue Per Available Room (RevPAR):** RevPAR, a key performance metric for hotels, saw significant declines. In Europe and North America, RevPAR fell by over 50% in 2020 compared to the previous year.
- **Business Adaptations:** Many hotels repurposed their facilities to serve as quarantine centers or accommodations for essential workers. The sector focused on implementing rigorous hygiene standards and flexible booking policies to attract and reassure guests as travel gradually resumed.

10.2.3 Cruises

The cruise industry came to a complete halt due to the pandemic:

- **Suspension of Operations:** Major cruise lines suspended operations globally, leading to massive financial losses and widespread layoffs. High-profile outbreaks on ships, such as the Diamond Princess, severely damaged the industry's reputation.
- **Economic Impact:** The cruise industry contributed significantly to the economies of port cities and coastal regions. The suspension of cruises resulted in substantial economic losses for

these communities.

- **Health and Safety Measures:** Upon resumption of operations, cruise lines implemented stringent health protocols, including mandatory testing, reduced passenger capacity, and modified itineraries. These measures aimed to rebuild consumer confidence and ensure the safety of passengers and crew.

10.3 Government Stimulus Packages

10.3.1 Types of Support

Governments worldwide introduced various stimulus packages and support measures to mitigate the economic impact on the tourism industry:

- **Financial Aid:** Direct financial assistance to businesses, including grants, loans, and subsidies, helped maintain liquidity and prevent bankruptcies. Examples include the Paycheck Protection Program (PPP) in the United States and furlough schemes in the United Kingdom.
- **Tax Relief:** Tax deferrals, reductions, and exemptions provided immediate financial relief to tourism-related businesses. This included deferred VAT payments, reduced corporate tax rates, and exemption from tourism-specific taxes.
- **Operational Support:** Measures to support operational continuity included subsidies for employee wages, rent relief, and utility cost reductions. Governments also facilitated access to credit and reduced regulatory burdens to help businesses survive the crisis.

10.3.2 Effectiveness and Challenges

- **Short-term Relief:** Government support measures provided essential short-term relief, preventing widespread bankruptcies and maintaining employment levels in the tourism sector.

- **Long-term Recovery:** The effectiveness of these measures in driving long-term recovery varied. Some countries faced challenges in efficiently distributing aid, while others struggled with the fiscal burden of prolonged support.
- **Innovation and Adaptation:** Governments encouraged innovation and adaptation within the tourism sector, promoting digital transformation, sustainable practices, and new business models to enhance resilience and competitiveness.

10.4 Case Studies of Tourism-Dependent Economies

10.4.1 Thailand

Thailand's economy heavily relies on tourism, accounting for approximately 20% of its GDP:

- **Economic Impact:** The pandemic led to a sharp contraction in Thailand's GDP, with the tourism sector bearing the brunt of the impact. The loss of international tourists caused widespread economic distress, particularly in popular tourist destinations like Bangkok, Phuket, and Chiang Mai.
- **Government Response:** The Thai government introduced a series of measures to support the tourism industry, including financial aid packages, tax relief, and domestic tourism promotion campaigns. Initiatives like the "We Travel Together"

program aimed to stimulate domestic travel and support local businesses.

- **Recovery Efforts:** Thailand focused on preparing for the return of international tourists with enhanced health protocols and marketing campaigns promoting the country as a safe destination. The introduction of special tourist visas and the development of travel bubbles were part of these efforts.

10.4.2 Greece

Greece, with tourism contributing around 25% of its GDP, faced severe economic challenges:

- **Economic Impact:** The pandemic caused a significant decline in tourist arrivals, leading to substantial revenue losses and increased unemployment in the tourism sector. Popular destinations such as Athens, Santorini, and Mykonos saw dramatic drops in visitor numbers.
- **Government Response:** The Greek government implemented a comprehensive support package, including financial aid, tax relief, and subsidies for businesses and workers in the tourism sector. Efforts to promote domestic tourism and extend the tourist season were also undertaken.
- **Recovery Efforts:** Greece launched marketing campaigns highlighting the country's safety and attractiveness as a tourist destination. The government collaborated with the private sector to implement health and safety protocols, ensuring a safe environment for visitors.

10.4.3 Maldives

The Maldives, with tourism accounting for over 30% of its GDP, experienced profound economic impacts:

- **Economic Impact:** The complete halt of international travel led to a severe economic downturn. The tourism-dependent economy faced significant revenue losses, and many resorts and businesses closed temporarily or permanently.

- **Government Response:** The Maldivian government introduced a range of measures to support the tourism industry, including financial aid, tax relief, and targeted support for SMEs. Efforts to promote domestic tourism and attract international tourists through marketing campaigns were intensified.
- **Recovery Efforts:** The Maldives implemented strict health protocols and promoted the country as a safe and exclusive destination. The government introduced special visa programs and incentives to attract long-stay tourists and remote workers.

10.5 Summary and Conclusions

The economic consequences of travel disruptions due to the COVID-19 pandemic were profound and far-reaching, affecting revenue, employment, and business operations across the tourism industry. Different sectors, such as aviation, hospitality, and cruises, faced unique challenges and adapted in various ways to survive the crisis. Government stimulus packages provided crucial support, but the long-term recovery required innovation, adaptation, and resilience. Case studies of tourism-dependent economies like Thailand, Greece, and the Maldives highlight the severe impacts and the efforts undertaken to revive and sustain the tourism sector. Moving forward, the industry must continue to build resilience, embrace innovation, and prepare for future disruptions to ensure sustainable growth and recovery.

CHAPTER TWELVE

GOVERNMENT AND INTERNATIONAL RESPONSES

12.1 Travel Restrictions and Quarantines

12.1.1 Imposition of Travel Restrictions

As COVID-19 rapidly spread across the globe, governments responded by implementing various travel restrictions aimed at containing the virus and protecting public health. These restrictions had significant implications for the tourism industry and global mobility.

- **Border Closures:** To limit the spread of COVID-19, many countries closed their borders entirely or partially, severely restricting international travel. This measure was one of the most immediate and dramatic responses, halting both inbound and outbound travel. Countries like Australia and New Zealand implemented stringent border closures early in the pandemic, which remained in place for extended periods.
- **Travel Bans:** Specific travel bans targeted travelers from high-risk countries. The criteria for these bans were often based on

infection rates and the presence of new variants. The United States, for instance, imposed travel bans on countries within the Schengen Area, the United Kingdom, China, and later, on South Africa and Brazil, among others.

- **Suspension of Visas:** Many countries suspended the issuance of tourist and business visas, impacting international mobility and tourism. For example, India suspended all existing visas, except for certain categories such as diplomatic and employment visas.
- **Domestic Travel Restrictions:** Within countries, domestic travel was also heavily restricted. Lockdowns and inter-state travel bans were implemented to curb the spread of the virus. In China, strict lockdown measures and travel restrictions within regions effectively contained the virus in its early stages.

12.1.2 Quarantine Measures

Quarantine measures were a cornerstone of travel policies during the pandemic, aimed at preventing the virus from spreading further.

- **Mandatory Quarantines:** Travelers entering many countries were required to undergo mandatory quarantine periods, typically ranging from 7 to 14 days. These quarantines were often enforced in government-designated facilities such as hotels, with costs borne by the travelers themselves. Countries like Taiwan and Hong Kong were strict with their quarantine enforcement, using electronic monitoring to ensure compliance.
- **Testing Requirements:** To minimize the risk of importing cases, many countries instituted testing requirements. Travelers often needed to present a negative COVID-19 test taken within a specified timeframe before departure, and some destinations required additional tests upon arrival. Iceland implemented a comprehensive testing protocol, where travelers underwent multiple tests during their quarantine period.
- **Health Monitoring:** Digital health forms and apps were introduced to track travelers' health status and ensure

compliance with quarantine and testing requirements. South Korea's extensive use of digital health monitoring allowed for effective tracking of potential cases and timely intervention.

12.1.3 Impact on Travel and Tourism

Travel restrictions and quarantine measures had far-reaching impacts on the travel and tourism industry, affecting both short-term operations and long-term recovery prospects.

- **Decline in Travel Volume:** International travel volumes plummeted as restrictions were imposed. The United Nations World Tourism Organization (UNWTO) reported a 74% decline in international tourist arrivals in 2020 compared to the previous year, resulting in a loss of over one billion international arrivals.
- **Traveler Behavior:** The inconvenience and uncertainty associated with travel restrictions deterred many potential travelers. Fear of sudden policy changes, such as unexpected quarantines or travel bans, led to a significant decline in consumer confidence. This, in turn, influenced travel behavior, with many opting to postpone or cancel trips.
- **Industry Response:** Travel businesses and destinations had to adapt quickly. Airlines, hotels, and tour operators introduced flexible booking policies, offering free cancellations or modifications to retain customer trust. Emphasis on health and safety measures, such as enhanced cleaning protocols and contactless services, became standard to reassure travelers.

12.2 Role of Organizations like WHO and CDC

12.2.1 World Health Organization (WHO)

The World Health Organization played a pivotal role in coordinating the global response to the COVID-19 pandemic, offering guidance and support to countries worldwide.

- **Guidance and Recommendations:** The WHO provided critical guidance on travel restrictions, health protocols, and preventive measures. Their recommendations were based on the latest scientific evidence and aimed at balancing public health protection with economic impacts. The WHO's International Health Regulations (IHR) provided a framework for managing public health risks without unnecessary interference with international traffic.
- **Coordination and Collaboration:** The WHO facilitated international cooperation and information sharing through regular updates, webinars, and technical support. This included the Strategic Preparedness and Response Plan (SPRP), which outlined key actions for countries to manage the pandemic.
- **Assessment and Advisories:** The WHO issued regular situation reports, risk assessments, and travel advisories. These communications helped governments and travelers make informed decisions based on the current epidemiological situation and emerging risks, such as new variants of the virus.

12.2.2 Centers for Disease Control and Prevention (CDC)

The CDC played a crucial role, particularly in the United States, by providing guidelines and recommendations to manage the pandemic.

- **Travel Health Notices:** The CDC issued travel health notices that categorized countries based on COVID-19 risk levels (Level 1: Low, Level 2: Moderate, Level 3: High, and Level 4: Very High). These notices guided travelers on the precautions to take and provided recommendations for high-risk countries.
- **Protocols and Guidelines:** The CDC developed comprehensive guidelines for various sectors, including airlines, cruise ships, and hotels. These guidelines covered a range of health and safety measures, from cleaning protocols and passenger screening to handling suspected cases of COVID-19.

- **Public Communication:** The CDC engaged in extensive public communication efforts, providing timely updates, educational materials, and resources. This included guidance on travel safety, vaccine information, and quarantine protocols, helping to inform and protect both travelers and the general public.

12.3 Case Studies of Effective Responses

12.3.1 New Zealand

New Zealand's approach to managing travel during the COVID-19 pandemic was highly effective and is often cited as a model response.

- **Early Action:** New Zealand acted swiftly by imposing strict border controls and mandatory quarantine measures for all incoming travelers early in the pandemic. This early intervention significantly reduced the importation of cases.
- **Comprehensive Testing and Tracing:** The country established robust testing and contact tracing systems. Mass testing and the use of the NZ COVID Tracer app enabled quick identification and isolation of cases, preventing community spread.
- **Clear Communication:** The New Zealand government maintained transparent and consistent communication with the public. Regular updates from Prime Minister Jacinda Ardern and health officials built trust and ensured compliance with health measures.
- **Success:** These measures resulted in low infection rates and allowed New Zealand to achieve periods of zero community transmission. The country managed to keep domestic tourism alive and later introduced the "Trans-Tasman Bubble" with Australia to restart international travel in a controlled manner.

12.3.2 South Korea

South Korea's effective use of technology and public cooperation played a significant role in managing travel and containing the virus.

- **Technology and Data:** South Korea leveraged advanced technology for contact tracing, including mobile apps and credit card transaction data. This allowed for accurate tracking of potential cases and timely interventions.
- **Testing and Quarantine:** Extensive testing and strict quarantine protocols for travelers minimized the risk of virus transmission from incoming passengers. Travelers were tested multiple times and monitored throughout their quarantine periods.
- **Public Cooperation:** High levels of public compliance with health guidelines, supported by clear and consistent government communication, were crucial to South Korea's success. The population's adherence to social distancing, mask-wearing, and hygiene practices helped control the spread of the virus.

12.3.3 Singapore

Singapore's strategic approach to travel management involved a combination of technology, clear protocols, and international collaboration.

- **Travel Corridors:** Singapore established reciprocal green lane arrangements with several countries, facilitating essential business and official travel. These arrangements involved mutual recognition of health protocols, reducing quarantine requirements for travelers.
- **Health Declarations:** The use of a comprehensive digital health declaration system enabled efficient screening and monitoring of travelers. The SafeTravel portal streamlined the process of entering Singapore and ensured compliance with health measures.
- **Vigilant Monitoring:** Continuous monitoring of global COVID-19 trends allowed Singapore to adapt its travel policies

rapidly. The government was proactive in adjusting travel advisories and implementing targeted measures based on the latest data.

12.4 Policy Harmonization

12.4.1 Importance of Harmonizing Travel Policies

The COVID-19 pandemic underscored the need for harmonized travel policies and health protocols to manage global health crises effectively.

- **Consistency:** Harmonized policies provide consistency, reducing confusion and facilitating smoother travel experiences. Uniform guidelines on testing, quarantine, and health measures help travelers navigate requirements across different countries, enhancing their confidence in international travel.
- **Safety and Trust:** Consistent policies build trust among travelers, ensuring a standardized approach to health and safety. This reduces the risk of virus transmission and fosters a sense of security, encouraging people to travel again.
- **Economic Recovery:** Coordinated policies support the recovery of the global tourism industry by encouraging travel and minimizing disruptions caused by varying regulations. A harmonized approach helps rebuild the travel ecosystem, benefiting airlines, hotels, and other tourism-related businesses.

12.4.2 Challenges to Harmonization

Achieving global policy harmonization presents several challenges:

- **Sovereignty:** Countries prioritize their sovereignty and public health priorities, leading to variations in travel policies. Each government responds to the pandemic based on its unique context, making it difficult to establish uniform standards.

- **Resource Disparities:** Differences in resources and healthcare infrastructure impact countries' ability to implement uniform measures. Developing countries may face challenges in adopting advanced technologies or comprehensive testing protocols.
- **Political Considerations:** Political dynamics and relationships between countries influence travel policies. Diplomatic tensions or differing political agendas can hinder efforts to harmonize travel protocols.

12.4.3 Steps Towards Harmonization

Despite the challenges, efforts to harmonize travel policies and protocols have been underway:

- **International Collaboration:** Organizations like the WHO, International Civil Aviation Organization (ICAO), and World Tourism Organization (UNWTO) facilitate dialogue and collaboration among countries. These organizations develop standardized guidelines and frameworks for managing travel during health crises.
- **Digital Solutions:** Digital health certificates and passports, such as the EU Digital COVID Certificate, provide a framework for harmonized health documentation. These solutions simplify cross-border travel by ensuring that travelers meet consistent health standards.
- **Bilateral Agreements:** Bilateral and multilateral agreements, such as travel bubbles and corridors, serve as initial steps towards broader policy harmonization. These agreements allow countries to align their protocols for mutual benefit, facilitating safer and more predictable travel.

12.5 Summary and Conclusions

Government and international responses to the COVID-19 pandemic involved a combination of travel restrictions, quarantine measures, and coordinated efforts by organizations like the WHO and CDC. Effective case studies from countries such as New Zealand, South Korea, and Singapore demonstrated the importance of early action, comprehensive testing and tracing, and clear communication. These measures helped manage travel during the pandemic and minimize the spread of the virus.

The pandemic highlighted the need for harmonizing travel policies globally. Consistent guidelines, international collaboration, and digital solutions play key roles in facilitating safe and seamless travel. Despite challenges such as sovereignty, resource disparities, and political considerations, efforts to harmonize travel protocols have been crucial in supporting the recovery and resilience of the global tourism industry.

The lessons learned from the COVID-19 pandemic will inform future strategies for managing travel during health crises. By adopting a coordinated and standardized approach, the tourism industry can better navigate future challenges and ensure a more resilient and sustainable future.

CHAPTER THIRTEEN

INDUSTRY ADAPTATIONS AND INNOVATIONS

Introduction

The COVID-19 pandemic has profoundly impacted the global tourism industry, necessitating a wave of adaptations and innovations to ensure safety, sustainability, and resilience. This chapter explores the various strategies and technological advancements that have emerged in response to the pandemic, highlighting the transformative effects on hygiene protocols, sustainability initiatives, contact tracing, health passports, and digital transformation within the travel sector.

13.1 Hygiene Protocols and Safety Measures

COVID-19 Prevention Hygiene Protocols

13.1.1 Enhanced Cleaning Procedures

Hotel and Accommodation Standards

The pandemic underscored the importance of cleanliness and hygiene in maintaining guest safety and confidence.

- **Increased Cleaning Frequency**: Hotels and other accommodation providers increased the frequency of cleaning and disinfection in public areas and guest rooms. High-touch surfaces, such as door handles, light switches, and elevator buttons, received particular attention.
- **Use of Hospital-Grade Disinfectants**: Many establishments adopted hospital-grade disinfectants and electrostatic sprayers to ensure thorough sanitation. These measures aimed to eliminate any potential traces of the virus and other pathogens.

Transportation Hygiene

Enhanced cleaning protocols were also implemented across various modes of transportation.

- **Airlines**: Airlines introduced rigorous cleaning procedures, including the disinfection of aircraft between flights. High-efficiency particulate air (HEPA) filters, capable of capturing viruses and bacteria, became standard in most aircraft.
- **Public Transport**: Buses, trains, and other public transportation systems increased cleaning schedules and employed advanced disinfection technologies, such as ultraviolet (UV) light, to sanitize vehicles and stations.

13.1.2 Social Distancing and Protective Measures
Physical Distancing

To minimize the risk of transmission, social distancing measures were widely adopted across the tourism industry.

- **Capacity Limits**: Hotels, restaurants, and tourist attractions implemented capacity limits to ensure adequate spacing between guests. This often involved reducing the number of available rooms, tables, and tour group sizes.
- **Queuing Systems**: New queuing systems were introduced to manage crowds and maintain physical distancing. Floor markers, barriers, and digital ticketing systems helped control the flow of visitors and reduce congestion.

Personal Protective Equipment (PPE)

The use of PPE became commonplace, protecting both staff and guests.

- **Masks and Face Shields**: Staff in hotels, restaurants, and transportation services were required to wear masks and face shields. Guests were also encouraged or mandated to wear masks in public areas.
- **Gloves and Sanitizers**: Hand sanitizers were made readily available in public spaces, and staff handling food or cleaning tasks often wore gloves to minimize direct contact.

13.1.3 Health Screenings and Testing
Temperature Checks
Temperature screenings became a standard procedure at entry points to detect potential cases of COVID-19.

- **Thermal Scanners**: Thermal scanners and handheld infrared thermometers were used to quickly screen large numbers of people. These devices helped identify individuals with elevated temperatures, a common symptom of the virus.
- **Contactless Thermometers**: Contactless thermometers minimized the risk of cross-contamination during screenings, ensuring a safer process for both staff and guests.

COVID-19 Testing
Testing played a crucial role in identifying and isolating infected individuals.

- **Pre-Travel Testing**: Many destinations required travelers to present a negative COVID-19 test result before arrival. This measure aimed to prevent the importation of the virus and protect local populations.
- **On-Site Testing**: Hotels and resorts offered on-site testing facilities, providing convenience for guests and ensuring compliance with travel requirements. Rapid antigen tests and PCR tests were commonly available.

13.2 Sustainability Initiatives
13.2.1 Environmental Awareness
Reduced Carbon Footprint
The pandemic highlighted the environmental impact of tourism, prompting a shift towards more sustainable practices.

- **Eco-Friendly Transportation**: Airlines and travel companies invested in more fuel-efficient aircraft and vehicles. The promotion of electric and hybrid transportation options gained traction as a means to reduce carbon emissions.

- **Sustainable Accommodations**: Hotels and resorts implemented energy-saving measures, such as LED lighting, solar panels, and water conservation systems. Sustainable design and construction practices became more prevalent, emphasizing the use of eco-friendly materials.

Conservation Efforts

Tourism operators increased their focus on conservation and the protection of natural resources.

- **Wildlife Protection**: The reduction in human activity during the pandemic allowed for the recovery of some wildlife populations. Tourism initiatives aimed at protecting endangered species and their habitats received renewed attention.
- **Marine Conservation**: Coastal and marine tourism operators implemented measures to reduce the impact on coral reefs and marine ecosystems. Efforts included promoting responsible diving practices and reducing plastic waste.

13.2.2 Community-Based Tourism
Supporting Local Economies

The pandemic underscored the importance of supporting local economies and communities.

- **Local Sourcing**: Hotels, restaurants, and tour operators increasingly sourced products and services locally, reducing their environmental footprint and supporting local businesses.
- **Cultural Preservation**: Community-based tourism initiatives focused on preserving cultural heritage and traditions. This approach not only provided authentic experiences for tourists but also generated income for local communities.

Fair Trade and Ethical Practices

Ethical tourism practices gained prominence, emphasizing fair trade and social responsibility.

- **Fair Wages**: Tourism businesses committed to paying fair wages to employees and ensuring safe working conditions. This focus on fair labor practices aimed to improve the livelihoods of those working in the tourism sector.
- **Ethical Wildlife Tourism**: Ethical wildlife tourism initiatives prioritized the well-being of animals and their natural habitats. This approach included avoiding activities that exploited animals for entertainment and promoting wildlife conservation.

13.2.3 Long-Term Sustainability Goals
Green Certification Programs

Green certification programs provided a framework for tourism businesses to achieve sustainability goals.

- **Certification Standards**: Programs such as Green Key, EarthCheck, and LEED (Leadership in Energy and Environmental Design) offered certification standards for eco-friendly practices. These standards covered areas such as energy efficiency, waste management, and water conservation.
- **Consumer Awareness**: Green certifications helped consumers identify and choose sustainable tourism options. This increased demand for environmentally responsible travel experiences encouraged more businesses to adopt sustainable practices.

Climate Action Plans

Tourism organizations developed comprehensive climate action plans to address the long-term impacts of climate change.

- **Carbon Offsetting**: Many companies introduced carbon offsetting programs, allowing travelers to compensate for their carbon emissions. Funds generated from these programs supported projects such as reforestation and renewable energy initiatives.

- **Sustainable Tourism Goals**: The United Nations World Tourism Organization (UNWTO) and other industry bodies set sustainable tourism goals, aiming to reduce carbon emissions, promote biodiversity, and enhance community resilience.

13.3 Contact Tracing and Health Passports
13.3.1 Implementation of Contact Tracing Apps
Development and Deployment

Governments and tech companies collaborated to develop and deploy contact tracing apps to track and manage the spread of COVID-19.

- **Bluetooth Technology**: Many contact tracing apps used Bluetooth technology to detect proximity between devices. If a user tested positive for COVID-19, the app would notify individuals who had been in close contact, advising them to self-isolate or get tested.
- **Data Privacy**: Ensuring data privacy and security was a major concern in the development of contact tracing apps. Many apps implemented decentralized data storage and anonymized user information to protect individual privacy.

Effectiveness and Challenges

The effectiveness of contact tracing apps varied, and several challenges emerged during implementation.

- **Adoption Rates**: The success of contact tracing apps depended on widespread adoption by the public. In many regions, uptake was lower than anticipated, reducing the apps' effectiveness in controlling outbreaks.
- **Technical Issues**: Technical challenges, such as compatibility with different operating systems and issues with battery consumption, affected the performance of some contact tracing apps.

13.3.2 Health Passports
Digital Health Credentials

Health passports, or digital health credentials, became a key tool in facilitating safe travel during the pandemic.

- **Vaccination Records**: Health passports provided a digital record of an individual's vaccination status, allowing travelers to prove they had received a COVID-19 vaccine. This was particularly important as many countries required proof of vaccination for entry.
- **Test Results**: In addition to vaccination records, health passports included results of COVID-19 tests, such as PCR or antigen tests. This information helped authorities verify that travelers were not carrying the virus.

Global Standards and Interoperability

Developing global standards and ensuring interoperability between different health passport systems were critical challenges.

- **Standardization Efforts**: Organizations like the International Air Transport Association (IATA) and the World Health Organization (WHO) worked to establish standardized health passport systems. These efforts aimed to create a uniform framework for verifying health credentials across borders.
- **Interoperability**: Ensuring that different health passport systems could communicate and exchange information was essential for seamless travel. Collaboration between governments, airlines, and technology providers was necessary to achieve interoperability.

13.3.3 Ethical and Privacy Considerations
Data Security

The use of contact tracing apps and health passports raised significant ethical and privacy concerns.

- **Data Protection**: Ensuring the security of personal health data was paramount. Robust data protection measures, such as encryption and secure storage, were implemented to safeguard user information.
- **User Consent**: Obtaining informed consent from users was crucial. Clear communication about how data would be used, stored, and shared helped build trust and encourage adoption.

Equity and Access

Addressing equity and access issues was critical to ensure that contact tracing and health passport systems were inclusive.

- **Digital Divide**: Access to smartphones and digital technology varied across populations, highlighting the need for alternative solutions for those without access. Providing physical health certificates or ensuring app compatibility with basic phones helped bridge the digital divide.
- **Ethical Use**: The ethical use of data and technology was a priority. Ensuring that health data was used solely for public health purposes and not for surveillance or discriminatory practices was essential to maintain public trust.

13.4 Digital Transformation and Contactless Travel
13.4.1 Acceleration of Digital Adoption
Remote Work and Virtual Meetings

The pandemic accelerated the adoption of digital technologies, reshaping the travel and tourism industry.

- **Remote Work**: The shift to remote work led to a decrease in business travel but also created new opportunities for digital nomads. Many destinations adapted by offering remote work visas and promoting themselves as ideal locations for remote workers.
- **Virtual Meetings**: The widespread use of virtual meeting platforms, such as Zoom and Microsoft Teams, reduced the need

for in-person conferences and meetings. This shift helped reduce the carbon footprint of business travel and promoted work-life balance.

Online Booking and Customer Service

Digital platforms played a crucial role in maintaining customer engagement and facilitating travel planning.

- **Online Booking Systems**: Travel companies enhanced their online booking systems, offering flexible cancellation policies and real-time updates on travel restrictions. These improvements helped build customer confidence and streamline the booking process.
- **Chatbots and AI**: The use of chatbots and artificial intelligence (AI) in customer service provided quick and efficient responses to traveler inquiries. AI-driven tools also assisted in personalizing travel recommendations based on user preferences.

13.4.2 Contactless Technologies

Touchless Check-In and Boarding

Contactless technologies became a cornerstone of safe and convenient travel.

- **Mobile Check-In**: Airlines and hotels widely adopted mobile check-in options, allowing travelers to complete the check-in process using their smartphones. This minimized physical contact and reduced waiting times.
- **Biometric Boarding**: Biometric technologies, such as facial recognition and fingerprint scanning, streamlined the boarding process at airports. These touchless systems improved security and efficiency while reducing the need for physical document handling.

Digital Payments

The pandemic accelerated the shift towards cashless transactions and digital payments.

- **Mobile Wallets**: Mobile payment platforms like Apple Pay, Google Wallet, and Samsung Pay gained popularity, offering a convenient and secure way to make purchases without physical contact.
- **QR Codes**: QR codes were used for a variety of purposes, including menu access in restaurants, contactless payments, and entry to attractions. This technology enabled seamless transactions and minimized the risk of virus transmission.

13.4.3 Virtual and Augmented Reality
Virtual Tours

Virtual and augmented reality technologies provided innovative ways to experience travel from home.

- **Virtual Museum Tours**: Many museums and cultural institutions offered virtual tours, allowing people to explore exhibits and collections online. This expanded access to cultural experiences and provided an alternative to physical visits.
- **Destination Previews**: Travel companies used virtual reality (VR) to offer immersive previews of destinations. Potential travelers could explore hotels, attractions, and landscapes in a virtual environment, aiding in travel planning and decision-making.

Augmented Reality Experiences

Augmented reality (AR) enhanced the travel experience by providing interactive and informative overlays.

- **Guided Tours**: AR applications enabled self-guided tours with interactive elements. Travelers could use their smartphones to access information, historical facts, and multimedia content about landmarks and attractions.

- **Navigation Assistance**: AR navigation tools provided real-time directions and information, helping travelers navigate unfamiliar destinations. This technology enhanced convenience and reduced the need for physical maps or guides.

The COVID-19 pandemic has driven significant adaptations and innovations within the tourism industry, fundamentally reshaping how we travel and experience destinations. Enhanced hygiene protocols, sustainability initiatives, contact tracing, health passports, and digital transformation have collectively contributed to a safer, more resilient, and sustainable travel ecosystem.

By exploring these industry adaptations and innovations, this chapter highlights the importance of proactive measures, technological advancements, and collaborative efforts in navigating the challenges posed by the pandemic. The lessons learned during this period will continue to influence the future of tourism, ensuring that the industry is better prepared to face future crises and meet the evolving needs of travelers worldwide.

CHAPTER FOURTEEN

Marketing and Communication Strategies

Introduction

The COVID-19 pandemic has profoundly disrupted the global tourism industry, necessitating a reevaluation of marketing and communication strategies. This chapter delves into the best practices for crisis management and communication, the importance of traveler assurance, the strategic use of social media to rebuild traveler confidence, and the promotion of safe destinations. By examining these aspects, we aim to provide a comprehensive understanding of how the tourism industry has adapted its marketing and communication strategies to navigate the challenges posed by the pandemic.

14.1 Crisis Management

14.1.1 Best Practices for Crisis Management

Preparedness and Risk Assessment

Effective crisis management begins with preparedness and thorough risk assessment.

- **Crisis Management Plans**: Tourism businesses must develop comprehensive crisis management plans that outline procedures for various scenarios, including health emergencies, natural disasters, and political unrest. These plans should be regularly updated and tested through drills and simulations.

- **Risk Assessment**: Conducting regular risk assessments helps identify potential threats and vulnerabilities. By understanding these risks, organizations can implement preventive measures and develop strategies to mitigate their impact.

Communication Protocols

Clear and consistent communication is crucial during a crisis.

- **Centralized Information**: Establish a centralized source of information to ensure that all stakeholders receive accurate and timely updates. This can be a dedicated website, a hotline, or a mobile app.
- **Transparency and Honesty**: Communicate openly and honestly with all stakeholders, including employees, travelers, and partners. Transparency builds trust and credibility, which are essential during a crisis.
- **Regular Updates**: Provide regular updates on the situation and the measures being taken to address it. Consistent communication helps manage expectations and reduces uncertainty.

Stakeholder Collaboration

Collaboration with stakeholders is vital for effective crisis management.

- **Government and Health Authorities**: Work closely with government and health authorities to align crisis response efforts with public health guidelines and regulations.
- **Industry Partners**: Collaborate with industry partners, such as airlines, hotels, and tour operators, to coordinate crisis response and share resources. Joint efforts can enhance the effectiveness of crisis management strategies.

- **Community Engagement**: Engage with local communities to understand their concerns and involve them in crisis response initiatives. Community support can strengthen resilience and recovery efforts.

14.1.2 Crisis Communication Strategies
Proactive Communication

Proactive communication helps manage the narrative and maintain control during a crisis.

- **Early Response**: Act quickly to acknowledge the crisis and communicate initial information. Early response demonstrates awareness and readiness to address the situation.
- **Key Messaging**: Develop clear and consistent key messages that address the concerns of different stakeholders. Tailor messages to specific audiences, such as travelers, employees, and partners, to ensure relevance and impact.
- **Media Relations**: Maintain strong relationships with the media to facilitate accurate and positive coverage. Provide regular press releases, hold press conferences, and offer spokesperson interviews to keep the media informed.

Social Media Engagement

Social media is a powerful tool for crisis communication.

- **Real-Time Updates**: Use social media platforms to provide real-time updates and address inquiries from the public. Quick responses to questions and concerns demonstrate responsiveness and care.
- **Hashtags and Campaigns**: Create dedicated hashtags and social media campaigns to unify crisis communication efforts. Encourage travelers and stakeholders to use these hashtags to share information and support recovery initiatives.
- **Influencer Partnerships**: Collaborate with social media influencers to amplify key messages and reach a broader

audience. Influencers can help convey safety measures, promote positive experiences, and rebuild traveler confidence.

Post-Crisis Communication

Post-crisis communication focuses on recovery and rebuilding trust.

- **Recovery Messaging**: Highlight recovery efforts and positive developments to shift the narrative from crisis to recovery. Share stories of resilience and success to inspire confidence.
- **Feedback and Evaluation**: Solicit feedback from stakeholders to evaluate the effectiveness of crisis communication efforts. Use this feedback to refine communication strategies and improve future crisis response.
- **Ongoing Engagement**: Maintain ongoing engagement with stakeholders even after the crisis has subsided. Regular updates on recovery progress and future plans help sustain trust and loyalty.

14.2 Traveler Assurance

14.2.1 Building Trust Through Safety Measures

Transparent Communication

Transparency is key to building traveler trust.

- **Health and Safety Protocols**: Clearly communicate the health and safety protocols implemented to protect travelers. This includes enhanced cleaning procedures, social distancing measures, and the use of personal protective equipment (PPE).
- **Certifications and Accreditations**: Highlight any certifications or accreditations received for meeting health and safety standards. Certifications from recognized bodies, such as the World Travel & Tourism Council's Safe Travels stamp, provide assurance to travelers.
- **Continuous Updates**: Provide continuous updates on the evolving situation and any changes to safety measures. Keeping

travelers informed about current conditions helps manage expectations and reduce anxiety.

Flexible Booking Policies

Flexibility in booking policies is essential to accommodate travelers' needs.

- **Cancellation Policies**: Offer flexible cancellation policies that allow travelers to modify or cancel bookings without incurring penalties. This flexibility encourages bookings and provides peace of mind.
- **Rescheduling Options**: Provide options for rescheduling trips in case of unexpected changes or travel restrictions. This allows travelers to adjust their plans without losing their investment.
- **Refund Guarantees**: Guarantee refunds for bookings affected by travel bans or health advisories. Clear and straightforward refund policies enhance traveler confidence and satisfaction.

14.2.2 Enhancing the Travel Experience
Personalized Communication

Personalized communication enhances the travel experience and builds trust.

- **Pre-Trip Communication**: Send personalized pre-trip communication to inform travelers about destination-specific safety measures and travel requirements. Tailored information helps travelers prepare and feel confident about their trip.
- **On-Trip Support**: Provide on-trip support through mobile apps, chatbots, and customer service hotlines. Real-time assistance ensures travelers have access to information and help whenever needed.
- **Post-Trip Engagement**: Engage with travelers post-trip to gather feedback and address any concerns. Positive post-trip communication reinforces trust and encourages repeat bookings.

Wellness and Wellbeing Initiatives

Focusing on wellness and wellbeing enhances the overall travel experience.

- **Wellness Programs**: Offer wellness programs and activities that promote physical and mental wellbeing. This can include yoga classes, meditation sessions, and spa treatments.
- **Healthy Dining Options**: Provide healthy dining options and highlight local cuisine that supports wellness. Emphasizing nutrition and health-conscious choices appeals to travelers seeking holistic experiences.
- **Stress-Free Environments**: Create stress-free environments by minimizing touchpoints and streamlining processes. Contactless check-in, digital payments, and virtual concierge services reduce friction and enhance convenience.

14.3 Leveraging Social Media

14.3.1 Communicating Safety Measures

Visual Content and Infographics

Visual content and infographics effectively communicate safety measures.

- **Instructional Videos**: Create instructional videos that demonstrate safety protocols, such as wearing masks, practicing social distancing, and using hand sanitizers. Visual demonstrations enhance understanding and compliance.
- **Infographics**: Develop infographics that summarize key safety measures and guidelines. Infographics are easily shareable and can reach a wide audience on social media platforms.
- **Behind-the-Scenes Content**: Share behind-the-scenes content that showcases the implementation of safety measures. Highlighting efforts by staff and management to ensure safety builds confidence among travelers.

Engaging Storytelling

Engaging storytelling humanizes safety measures and makes them more relatable.

- **Staff Stories**: Share stories and testimonials from staff members about their commitment to maintaining safety. Personal stories create an emotional connection and reinforce the importance of safety protocols.
- **Traveler Experiences**: Highlight positive traveler experiences that emphasize safety and satisfaction. User-generated content, such as photos and reviews, provides authentic perspectives and builds trust.
- **Virtual Tours**: Offer virtual tours of destinations, hotels, and attractions to showcase safety measures in action. Virtual tours provide a glimpse of the travel experience and reassure potential travelers.

14.3.2 Rebuilding Traveler Confidence
Influencer Collaborations

Collaborating with influencers helps rebuild traveler confidence.

- **Authentic Endorsements**: Partner with influencers who align with the brand's values and can authentically endorse safety measures. Influencers' trusted voices can sway potential travelers and boost confidence.
- **Safety Campaigns**: Launch safety campaigns with influencers to highlight key messages and initiatives. Influencers can create content that educates their followers about safe travel practices and encourages responsible behavior.
- **Interactive Engagement**: Use influencers to engage with the audience through live sessions, Q&A sessions, and interactive content. Direct interactions with influencers allow travelers to ask questions and receive real-time responses.

User-Generated Content

User-generated content (UGC) serves as powerful social proof.

- **Encouraging Reviews**: Encourage travelers to share their experiences and leave reviews on social media platforms and travel websites. Positive reviews and testimonials from fellow travelers enhance credibility and trust.
- **Photo and Video Contests**: Organize photo and video contests that encourage travelers to showcase their safe travel experiences. Contests create a sense of community and generate engaging UGC.
- **Sharing UGC**: Actively share UGC on official social media channels. Highlighting real traveler experiences reinforces the message of safety and satisfaction.

14.4 Promoting Safe Destinations
14.4.1 Highlighting Safety Protocols
Destination-Specific Campaigns
Destination-specific campaigns focus on safety protocols and measures.

- **Safety Certifications**: Highlight destinations that have received safety certifications and accreditations. Promoting these certifications assures travelers of the destination's commitment to health and safety.
- **Local Health Guidelines**: Communicate local health guidelines and regulations to inform travelers about what to expect. Clear and concise information helps travelers feel prepared and confident.
- **Collaborative Campaigns**: Collaborate with local tourism boards, hotels, and attractions to create unified safety campaigns. Joint efforts amplify the message and enhance visibility.

Interactive Content

Interactive content engages travelers and provides valuable information.

- **Interactive Maps**: Create interactive maps that highlight safe destinations, attractions, and accommodations. Maps can include information on safety protocols, health facilities, and travel advisories.
- **Virtual Experiences**: Offer virtual experiences, such as live streaming of events, virtual tours, and interactive webinars. Virtual experiences allow travelers to explore destinations from the comfort of their homes.
- **Safety Quizzes**: Develop safety quizzes that test travelers' knowledge of safety protocols and guidelines. Quizzes are engaging and educational, reinforcing the importance of safe travel practices.

14.4.2 Campaigns and Partnerships
Collaborative Marketing

Collaborative marketing efforts strengthen the promotion of safe destinations.

- **Joint Promotions**: Partner with airlines, hotels, and tour operators to offer joint promotions and packages. Collaborative promotions provide added value and convenience for travelers.
- **Destination Partnerships**: Establish partnerships with other destinations to promote safe travel corridors. Coordinated efforts between destinations enhance traveler confidence and encourage cross-border travel.
- **Industry Alliances**: Join industry alliances and associations that advocate for safe travel. Collective advocacy amplifies the message and influences policy decisions.

Digital Campaigns

Digital campaigns leverage online platforms to reach a wide audience.

- **Targeted Advertising**: Use targeted advertising to reach specific demographics and traveler segments. Personalized ads that emphasize safety measures and benefits resonate with potential travelers.
- **Social Media Campaigns**: Launch social media campaigns that highlight safe destinations and experiences. Use engaging content, such as videos, stories, and polls, to capture attention and drive engagement.
- **Email Marketing**: Implement email marketing campaigns to provide updates, offers, and safety information. Personalized emails foster a direct connection with travelers and keep them informed.

The COVID-19 pandemic has necessitated significant adaptations in marketing and communication strategies within the tourism industry. By embracing best practices in crisis management, providing traveler assurance, leveraging social media, and promoting safe destinations, the industry can navigate the challenges posed by the pandemic and rebuild traveler confidence.

This chapter has explored the importance of proactive communication, stakeholder collaboration, and transparency in crisis management. It has highlighted the role of personalized communication, wellness initiatives, and flexible booking policies in enhancing the travel experience. Additionally, it has examined the power of social media, influencer collaborations, and user-generated content in rebuilding traveler confidence. Finally, it has emphasized the importance of promoting safe destinations through destination-specific campaigns, interactive content, and collaborative marketing efforts.

As the tourism industry continues to evolve, these strategies will remain crucial in ensuring a safe, resilient, and sustainable future for travel. By prioritizing health and safety, fostering trust, and embracing innovation, the industry can emerge stronger and more prepared for future challenges.

CHAPTER FIFTEEN

BUILDING RESILIENCE IN THE TOURISM INDUSTRY

Introduction

The tourism industry has faced numerous challenges from various outbreaks, each imparting valuable lessons. Building resilience in the tourism sector requires a comprehensive approach, leveraging past experiences, fostering cross-sector collaboration, engaging in scenario planning, and implementing strategies for future preparedness. This chapter explores these elements in depth, providing insights into how the industry can strengthen its resilience against future crises.

15.1 Lessons Learned from Past Outbreaks

15.1.1 Analysis of Historical Outbreaks

SARS (Severe Acute Respiratory Syndrome)

The SARS outbreak of 2002-2003 highlighted several critical areas for improvement in the tourism industry:

- **Rapid Response**: The swift spread of SARS demonstrated the need for rapid response mechanisms. Delays in acknowledging and addressing the outbreak exacerbated its impact.

- **Communication Failures**: Inconsistent and unclear communication from authorities and industry stakeholders led to widespread confusion and fear among travelers.
- **Impact on Trust**: The lack of transparent information eroded public trust, making recovery efforts more challenging.

H1N1 Influenza (Swine Flu)

The H1N1 outbreak in 2009 further underscored the importance of preparedness:

- **Health Protocols**: The importance of implementing and adhering to strict health protocols, including hygiene and vaccination campaigns, was evident.
- **Coordination**: Effective coordination between the tourism industry and health authorities played a crucial role in managing the outbreak.
- **Economic Resilience**: The economic impact highlighted the need for financial resilience strategies, including support for affected businesses and employees.

Ebola Outbreak

The Ebola outbreaks, particularly in West Africa, provided lessons on managing fear and misinformation:

- **Localized Impact**: The outbreak's localized nature emphasized the importance of targeted responses and support for affected regions.
- **Media Influence**: Media coverage significantly influenced public perception and travel behavior, underscoring the need for accurate and responsible reporting.
- **Health Infrastructure**: Weak health infrastructures in affected regions demonstrated the critical need for investment in healthcare systems.

15.1.2 Common Themes and Takeaways

Analyzing these outbreaks reveals common themes and takeaways that can inform future resilience-building efforts:

- **Proactive Preparedness**: Proactive measures, including scenario planning and early detection systems, are essential for mitigating the impact of outbreaks.
- **Transparent Communication**: Clear, consistent, and transparent communication is crucial for maintaining public trust and managing fear.
- **Cross-Sector Collaboration**: Collaboration between the tourism industry, health authorities, and other stakeholders is vital for effective crisis management.
- **Economic Support**: Financial resilience strategies, including government support and insurance mechanisms, are necessary to protect businesses and employees.

15.2 Cross-Sector Collaboration
15.2.1 Importance of Collaboration
Coordinated Efforts

Collaboration between the tourism industry and public health sectors ensures coordinated efforts in managing outbreaks:

- **Resource Sharing**: Sharing resources, such as medical supplies, expertise, and information, enhances the ability to respond effectively.
- **Unified Messaging**: Coordinated messaging from health authorities and tourism stakeholders provides consistent information to the public, reducing confusion and panic.
- **Joint Strategies**: Developing joint strategies for outbreak response ensures that health measures align with tourism operations, minimizing disruptions.

Building Trust

Collaboration builds trust between stakeholders, essential for effective crisis management:

- **Stakeholder Engagement**: Engaging all stakeholders, including local communities, travelers, and industry players, fosters a sense of shared responsibility and cooperation.
- **Public-Private Partnerships**: Public-private partnerships leverage the strengths of both sectors, enhancing the overall response capability.

15.2.2 Case Studies of Successful Collaboration

Singapore: A Model of Coordination

During the SARS outbreak, Singapore demonstrated exemplary coordination between its tourism and health sectors:

- **Integrated Command Structure**: An integrated command structure facilitated rapid decision-making and implementation of health measures.
- **Public Communication**: Transparent and consistent communication from authorities helped manage public fear and maintain trust.
- **Economic Support**: The government provided financial support to affected businesses, aiding in the swift recovery of the tourism sector.

South Korea: Effective Use of Technology

South Korea's response to the COVID-19 pandemic highlighted the role of technology in cross-sector collaboration:

- **Contact Tracing**: Advanced contact tracing systems, developed in collaboration with the tech industry, played a crucial role in containing the virus.
- **Public Health Communication**: Effective use of digital platforms ensured timely dissemination of information to the public.
- **Travel Regulations**: Coordinated efforts between health authorities and the tourism industry ensured that travel regulations were implemented smoothly, minimizing

disruptions.

15.3 Scenario Planning
15.3.1 Role of Scenario Planning
Preparing for Uncertainty

Scenario planning involves preparing for various possible futures, allowing the tourism industry to anticipate and respond to different outbreak scenarios:

- **Risk Identification**: Identifying potential risks and their impacts enables the development of targeted response strategies.
- **Flexible Planning**: Scenario planning promotes flexible planning, allowing for quick adaptation to changing circumstances.
- **Resource Allocation**: Anticipating different scenarios helps allocate resources effectively, ensuring readiness for various outcomes.

Enhancing Resilience

Scenario planning enhances resilience by fostering a proactive approach to crisis management:

- **Simulations and Drills**: Regular simulations and drills help test and refine response plans, ensuring that stakeholders are prepared for real-world scenarios.
- **Stakeholder Involvement**: Involving all stakeholders in scenario planning promotes a collaborative approach, enhancing overall resilience.
- **Learning from Experience**: Incorporating lessons learned from past outbreaks into scenario planning ensures that strategies are continually improved.

15.3.2 Implementing Scenario Planning
Steps for Effective Scenario Planning

Implementing effective scenario planning involves several key steps:

- **Risk Assessment**: Conduct thorough risk assessments to identify potential outbreak scenarios and their impacts on the tourism industry.
- **Scenario Development**: Develop multiple scenarios, ranging from best-case to worst-case, to cover a wide range of possibilities.
- **Action Plans**: Create detailed action plans for each scenario, outlining specific measures and responsibilities.
- **Regular Review**: Regularly review and update scenarios and action plans to ensure they remain relevant and effective.

Case Studies of Successful Scenario Planning
The World Travel & Tourism Council (WTTC)
The WTTC has been at the forefront of promoting scenario planning in the tourism industry:

- **Scenario-Based Reports**: The WTTC publishes scenario-based reports that outline potential future scenarios and their implications for the tourism industry.
- **Global Collaboration**: Collaborating with industry stakeholders, governments, and health authorities, the WTTC promotes a coordinated approach to scenario planning.

Tourism Australia
Tourism Australia's proactive scenario planning efforts have strengthened its resilience:

- **Market Analysis**: Regular market analysis helps Tourism Australia anticipate changes in travel patterns and adapt its strategies accordingly.
- **Stakeholder Engagement**: Engaging stakeholders in scenario planning ensures a collaborative approach to crisis management.

15.4 Strategies for Future Preparedness

15.4.1 Health and Safety Protocols

Strengthening Health Infrastructure

Investing in health infrastructure is critical for future preparedness:

- **Healthcare Facilities**: Enhancing healthcare facilities, including hospitals and clinics, ensures that the healthcare system can handle future outbreaks.
- **Training and Development**: Providing training and development for healthcare workers equips them with the skills needed to manage outbreaks effectively.
- **Resource Availability**: Ensuring the availability of essential resources, such as medical supplies and PPE, enhances preparedness.

Implementing Robust Protocols

Robust health and safety protocols are essential for protecting travelers and staff:

- **Hygiene Standards**: Implementing and maintaining high hygiene standards in tourism facilities, including hotels, airports, and attractions, minimizes the risk of infection.
- **Health Screenings**: Regular health screenings for travelers and staff help detect and manage potential outbreaks early.
- **Vaccination Campaigns**: Promoting vaccination campaigns for travelers and staff enhances overall health resilience.

15.4.2 Technology and Innovation

Leveraging Technology

Technology plays a crucial role in enhancing preparedness and response capabilities:

- **Digital Health Passports**: Implementing digital health passports enables travelers to provide proof of vaccination and test results, facilitating safe travel.

- **Contact Tracing Apps**: Developing and deploying contact tracing apps helps track and manage outbreaks effectively.
- **AI and Data Analytics**: Leveraging AI and data analytics enhances the ability to predict and respond to outbreaks, improving overall preparedness.

Innovation in Crisis Management

Innovation drives improvements in crisis management strategies:

- **Real-Time Monitoring**: Implementing real-time monitoring systems provides up-to-date information on outbreaks, enabling timely responses.
- **Virtual Reality Training**: Using virtual reality for training simulations prepares staff for various outbreak scenarios, enhancing their readiness.
- **Remote Services**: Offering remote services, such as virtual tours and online customer support, ensures continuity of operations during crises.

15.4.3 Financial Resilience

Supporting Businesses

Supporting tourism businesses enhances their financial resilience:

- **Government Support**: Providing financial support, including grants and loans, helps businesses navigate crises and recover more quickly.
- **Insurance Mechanisms**: Developing insurance mechanisms that cover outbreak-related losses provides financial protection for businesses.
- **Diversification**: Encouraging diversification of revenue streams reduces dependence on specific markets, enhancing overall resilience.

Protecting Employees

Protecting employees is essential for maintaining a resilient workforce:

- **Job Security**: Ensuring job security through government support and business continuity plans helps retain skilled workers.
- **Mental Health Support**: Providing mental health support services helps employees cope with the stress and challenges of crises.
- **Training and Development**: Offering training and development opportunities equips employees with the skills needed to manage future outbreaks.

15.4.4 Community Engagement

Building Community Resilience

Engaging local communities strengthens overall resilience:

- **Community Health Initiatives**: Promoting community health initiatives enhances public health resilience, benefiting both residents and travelers.
- **Local Partnerships**: Establishing partnerships with local organizations ensures a coordinated approach to crisis management.
- **Public Education**: Educating the public on health and safety measures fosters a culture of preparedness and cooperation.

Enhancing Public Trust

Building and maintaining public trust is crucial for effective crisis management:

- **Transparent Communication**: Providing clear, consistent, and transparent information builds trust and reduces fear.
- **Community Involvement**: Involving communities in decision-making processes fosters a sense of ownership and cooperation.

- **Cultural Sensitivity**: Ensuring that health and safety measures are culturally sensitive enhances public acceptance and compliance.

Building resilience in the tourism industry requires a multifaceted approach, incorporating lessons learned from past outbreaks, fostering cross-sector collaboration, engaging in scenario planning, and implementing strategies for future preparedness. By strengthening health infrastructure, leveraging technology, enhancing financial resilience, and engaging communities, the tourism industry can better navigate future crises and ensure a safe, sustainable, and resilient future for travel.

This chapter has explored the importance of learning from historical outbreaks, the role of cross-sector collaboration, the benefits of scenario planning, and strategies for future preparedness. As the tourism industry continues to evolve, these elements will remain crucial in building resilience and ensuring that the industry is well-prepared to face future challenges. By prioritizing health and safety, fostering trust, and embracing innovation, the tourism industry can emerge stronger and more resilient in the face of future crises.

CHAPTER SIXTEEN

THE ROLE OF TECHNOLOGY IN FUTURE TRAVEL

The rapid advancement of technology is reshaping the future of travel, offering innovative solutions to enhance safety, efficiency, and the overall travel experience. This chapter delves into the role of technology in future travel, focusing on predictive analytics and health monitoring, innovations in travel technology, artificial intelligence, and biometric technology. These advancements are not only transforming how we travel but also playing a crucial role in managing health risks and improving security.

16.1 Predictive Analytics and Health Monitoring

16.1.1 Predictive Analytics

Enhancing Travel Safety

Predictive analytics involves the use of data, statistical algorithms, and machine learning techniques to identify the likelihood of future outcomes based on historical data. In the context of travel, predictive analytics can significantly enhance safety and efficiency:

- **Risk Assessment**: Predictive models can assess potential health risks in different destinations by analyzing data from various sources, including epidemiological reports, climate conditions, and traveler health records. This enables travelers and authorities to make informed decisions about travel plans. For instance, during the COVID-19 pandemic, predictive analytics helped identify hotspots and potential risk areas, allowing travelers to avoid these regions and authorities to implement targeted restrictions.

- **Flight Safety**: Airlines can use predictive analytics to anticipate maintenance needs, identify potential mechanical issues, and optimize flight routes for safety and efficiency. This reduces the risk of in-flight emergencies and ensures smoother operations. Predictive maintenance can foresee and address potential problems before they occur, minimizing delays and enhancing passenger safety.
- **Crowd Management**: By analyzing patterns in traveler behavior and movement, predictive analytics can help manage crowds at airports, tourist attractions, and events. This minimizes congestion and reduces the risk of virus transmission. For example, data-driven insights can help airports allocate resources more effectively, ensuring that security and check-in lines move smoothly even during peak travel times.

Personalized Travel Experiences

Predictive analytics also enables the personalization of travel experiences:

- **Tailored Recommendations**: Travel companies can use predictive analytics to provide personalized recommendations for destinations, accommodations, and activities based on travelers' preferences, past behavior, and current trends. This personalization enhances the travel experience by aligning it with individual interests and needs.
- **Dynamic Pricing**: Predictive models can help airlines and hotels optimize pricing strategies based on demand forecasts, ensuring competitive rates and maximizing revenue. By analyzing

historical booking patterns and current market conditions, businesses can adjust prices in real-time to attract more customers while maximizing profits.

- **Travel Itineraries**: By analyzing data on traveler preferences and local conditions, predictive analytics can create customized travel itineraries that enhance the overall travel experience. For example, if a traveler prefers cultural experiences and fine dining, the itinerary can highlight museums, historical sites, and top-rated restaurants.

16.1.2 Health Monitoring
Real-Time Health Data

Health monitoring technology is becoming increasingly integral to travel safety:

- **Wearable Devices**: Wearable health devices, such as smartwatches and fitness trackers, can monitor vital signs in real-time, including heart rate, temperature, and oxygen levels. This data can be shared with healthcare providers to detect potential health issues early. During the COVID-19 pandemic, such devices played a crucial role in monitoring symptoms and ensuring timely medical intervention.
- **Health Apps**: Mobile health apps can track symptoms, provide health advice, and connect travelers with medical professionals. These apps can also integrate with contact tracing systems to monitor potential exposure to infectious diseases. For instance, apps like "Travel Safe" and "Health Passport" not only track health status but also provide real-time updates on local health advisories and restrictions.
- **Remote Health Monitoring**: For travelers with chronic conditions, remote health monitoring systems allow continuous monitoring of health status and remote consultations with healthcare providers, ensuring timely intervention if needed. This is particularly beneficial for elderly travelers or those with conditions that require regular medical attention.

Enhancing Public Health Response

Health monitoring technology plays a crucial role in public health response during outbreaks:

- **Early Detection**: Real-time health monitoring enables the early detection of symptoms, allowing for swift isolation and treatment of infected individuals to prevent the spread of disease. For example, temperature screening at airports can quickly identify travelers with fever, a common symptom of many infectious diseases.
- **Data Integration**: Integrating health data from various sources, such as wearables, health apps, and public health databases, provides a comprehensive view of the health landscape, aiding in the identification and management of outbreaks. This integrated approach allows for more accurate and timely public health responses.
- **Travel Health Passports**: Digital health passports can store and verify travelers' health information, including vaccination records and test results. These passports facilitate safe travel by ensuring that only healthy individuals are allowed to travel. For instance, the European Union's Digital COVID Certificate enabled safe travel across member states by providing proof of vaccination, testing, or recovery from COVID-19.

16.2 Innovations in Travel Technology

16.2.1 Contactless Travel

Reducing Physical Contact

The COVID-19 pandemic has accelerated the adoption of contactless technologies in travel:

- **Mobile Check-In**: Mobile apps enable travelers to check-in for flights, hotels, and other services without physical interaction, reducing the risk of virus transmission. This contactless approach not only enhances safety but also improves convenience by allowing travelers to bypass long lines at check-in counters.

- **Digital Payments**: Contactless payment systems, such as mobile wallets and QR code payments, minimize the need for cash handling and physical contact with payment terminals. This technology enhances hygiene and speeds up transactions, making the travel experience more seamless.
- **Self-Service Kiosks**: Airports and hotels are increasingly using self-service kiosks for check-in, baggage drop, and information services, enhancing efficiency and safety. These kiosks reduce the need for direct human interaction, thereby minimizing the risk of virus spread.

Enhancing Convenience

Contactless technologies also enhance the convenience and efficiency of travel:

- **Digital Boarding Passes**: Digital boarding passes can be stored on mobile devices, eliminating the need for paper tickets and streamlining the boarding process. This not only reduces environmental impact but also speeds up the boarding process, allowing for more efficient flight operations.
- **Keyless Entry**: Hotels are adopting keyless entry systems that allow guests to use their smartphones to unlock their rooms, providing a seamless check-in experience. This technology enhances guest satisfaction by reducing wait times and offering a modern, tech-savvy experience.
- **Smart Luggage**: Smart luggage equipped with GPS tracking and digital locks offers added convenience and security for travelers. These innovative suitcases can be tracked via mobile apps, ensuring that travelers always know the whereabouts of their belongings.

16.2.2 Virtual and Augmented Reality
Transforming Travel Experiences

Virtual and augmented reality (VR and AR) technologies are transforming how travelers experience destinations:

- **Virtual Tours**: VR technology enables travelers to take virtual tours of destinations, attractions, and accommodations, allowing them to explore and plan their trips from the comfort of their homes. This immersive experience can inspire travelers to visit new places and make informed decisions about their itineraries.
- **Augmented Reality Guides**: AR apps provide interactive guides that overlay information on real-world environments, enhancing the travel experience with historical facts, navigation assistance, and cultural insights. For example, pointing a smartphone at a historic monument can display information about its history and significance.
- **Immersive Experiences**: VR and AR create immersive travel experiences, such as virtual safaris, underwater explorations, and historical reenactments, offering new ways to experience destinations. These technologies can also provide accessibility to those who may not be able to travel physically.

Enhancing Marketing and Engagement

VR and AR technologies are also valuable marketing tools for the travel industry:

- **Destination Marketing**: Tourism boards and travel companies use VR and AR to showcase destinations and attractions, providing potential travelers with a taste of what they can expect. This immersive marketing approach can significantly boost interest and bookings.
- **Interactive Advertising**: AR-enabled advertisements allow travelers to interact with promotional content, creating engaging and memorable marketing experiences. For instance, an AR ad for a travel destination might let users explore landmarks in 3D, enhancing their engagement.

- **Travel Planning**: VR and AR tools help travelers visualize and plan their trips, enhancing the decision-making process and boosting confidence in travel choices. Virtual hotel tours, for example, can help travelers choose accommodations that best meet their needs.

16.3 Artificial Intelligence and Predictive Analytics
16.3.1 AI in Travel Health Management
Early Detection and Response

Artificial intelligence (AI) and predictive analytics play a crucial role in managing travel health risks:

- **Disease Surveillance**: AI algorithms analyze data from multiple sources, including health records, social media, and news reports, to detect early signs of disease outbreaks and predict their spread. This allows health authorities to implement preventive measures and travelers to adjust their plans accordingly.
- **Predictive Models**: Predictive analytics models use historical data and real-time inputs to forecast the trajectory of outbreaks, enabling timely interventions and resource allocation. These models can help governments and health organizations prepare for potential spikes in cases and allocate resources more effectively.
- **Symptom Analysis**: AI-powered health apps analyze symptoms reported by travelers to identify potential cases of infectious diseases and recommend appropriate actions. For example, if a traveler reports symptoms consistent with COVID-19, the app can suggest getting tested and self-isolating until results are confirmed.

Personalized Health Recommendations

AI enhances the personalization of health recommendations for travelers:

- **Risk Assessment**: AI systems assess individual health risks based on factors such as age, medical history, and travel itinerary, providing personalized health advice and precautions. This tailored approach ensures that travelers receive relevant and accurate health information.
- **Health Monitoring**: AI-powered wearable devices continuously monitor vital signs and provide real-time health alerts, ensuring travelers can address health issues promptly. These devices can also offer personalized health tips based on the user's current condition and travel plans.
- **Travel Insurance**: AI algorithms help travel insurance providers assess risk levels and customize coverage plans based on travelers' health profiles and destinations. This ensures that travelers receive adequate coverage while minimizing costs for insurers.

16.3.2 AI in Travel Operations
Enhancing Efficiency and Safety

AI optimizes travel operations, enhancing efficiency and safety:

- **Flight Operations**: AI systems analyze weather data, air traffic, and aircraft performance to optimize flight routes, reduce delays, and improve fuel efficiency. This not only saves costs for airlines but also ensures a smoother travel experience for passengers.
- **Baggage Handling**: AI-powered baggage handling systems track luggage in real-time, reducing the risk of lost or delayed baggage and enhancing the passenger experience. These systems can also optimize baggage routing, ensuring that bags arrive at their destination on time.
- **Security Screening**: AI technology enhances security screening processes by analyzing passenger data and identifying potential threats, ensuring safe and efficient travel. For instance, AI can help screen large volumes of passengers quickly while maintaining high security standards.

Improving Customer Service

AI revolutionizes customer service in the travel industry:

- **Chatbots**: AI-powered chatbots provide 24/7 customer support, answering queries, assisting with bookings, and resolving issues in real-time. These chatbots can handle multiple languages and provide consistent, accurate information to travelers.
- **Personalized Recommendations**: AI algorithms analyze traveler preferences and behavior to offer personalized recommendations for destinations, activities, and accommodations. This enhances the travel experience by aligning it with individual interests.
- **Language Translation**: AI-powered language translation apps facilitate communication between travelers and locals, enhancing the travel experience in foreign destinations. These apps can translate text, speech, and even images, making it easier for travelers to navigate and interact in different cultures.

16.4 Biometric Technology

16.4.1 Enhancing Travel Security

Biometric Identification

Biometric technology enhances travel security through reliable identification methods:

- **Facial Recognition**: Facial recognition systems match travelers' faces with their passport photos, ensuring accurate and efficient identity verification at airports and border crossings. This technology reduces the risk of identity fraud and speeds up the verification process.
- **Fingerprint Scanning**: Fingerprint scanning provides a secure and convenient method for identity verification, reducing the risk of fraudulent travel documents. This biometric method is widely used in visa applications and border controls to ensure that the person presenting the document is the legitimate holder.

- **Iris Scanning**: Iris scanning offers a highly accurate and secure biometric identification method, enhancing the efficiency of security screening processes. This technology is less intrusive than other methods and provides a high level of accuracy.

Streamlining Border Control

Biometric technology streamlines border control processes:

- **Automated Border Gates**: Automated border gates equipped with biometric scanners expedite the entry and exit process, reducing wait times and enhancing security. These gates can process travelers quickly and accurately, ensuring a smooth flow through immigration.
- **E-Visa Systems**: Biometric e-visa systems enable travelers to apply for and receive visas electronically, simplifying the application process and enhancing security. This reduces the need for physical documents and in-person visits to embassies or consulates.
- **Enhanced Screening**: Biometric technology enhances the accuracy and efficiency of security screenings, reducing the risk of unauthorized entry and improving overall border control. This technology ensures that only legitimate travelers are granted entry, enhancing national security.

16.4.2 Improving Travel Efficiency

Seamless Travel Experience

Biometric technology creates a seamless travel experience:

- **Single Token Travel**: Biometric systems enable single token travel, where travelers use a single biometric identifier (e.g., facial recognition) for all checkpoints, from check-in to boarding. This streamlines the travel process, reducing the need for multiple documents and verification steps.
- **Personalized Services**: Biometric technology allows for personalized services, such as customized check-in experiences

and targeted promotions, enhancing the overall travel experience. For instance, facial recognition can enable personalized greetings and services at hotels and airports.

- **Contactless Interactions**: Biometric systems reduce the need for physical contact during identity verification and security checks, enhancing safety and convenience. This is particularly important in the post-pandemic world, where minimizing contact is crucial for preventing the spread of infectious diseases.

Enhancing Airport Operations

Biometric technology optimizes airport operations:

- **Passenger Flow Management**: Biometric systems track passenger movement through airports, helping manage crowds and optimize resource allocation. This ensures that airports can handle high volumes of passengers efficiently, reducing congestion and wait times.
- **Security Efficiency**: Biometric technology enhances the efficiency of security screening processes, reducing wait times and improving the passenger experience. This allows airports to maintain high security standards while providing a smooth and hassle-free experience for travelers.
- **Operational Insights**: Biometric data provides valuable insights into passenger behavior and airport operations, enabling continuous improvement and optimization. This data can be used to enhance airport services, streamline processes, and improve overall efficiency.

The role of technology in future travel is transformative, offering innovative solutions to enhance safety, efficiency, and the overall travel experience. Predictive analytics and health monitoring provide valuable insights into travel risks and enable personalized health recommendations. Innovations in travel technology, including contactless travel and virtual reality, enhance convenience and engagement. Artificial intelligence and predictive analytics revolutionize travel health management and operations, while biometric technology enhances travel security and efficiency. As technology continues to advance, its integration into the travel industry will be crucial in ensuring a safe, seamless, and resilient future for travel.

CHAPTER SEVENTEEN

SUSTAINABLE TOURISM POST-PANDEMIC

Introduction

The COVID-19 pandemic profoundly impacted the global tourism industry, presenting an opportunity to re-evaluate and transform tourism practices towards a more sustainable future. This chapter explores sustainable tourism post-pandemic, focusing on balancing tourism growth and public health, community-based tourism, eco-friendly certifications, and promoting eco-friendly and responsible travel. The pandemic highlighted the need for a more resilient and environmentally conscious approach to tourism, emphasizing the importance of sustainable practices for the industry's long-term viability.

17.1 Balancing Tourism Growth and Public Health

17.1.1 Understanding the Interconnection

Tourism and Public Health

The relationship between tourism and public health has always been intertwined, but the pandemic underscored its critical importance. Balancing tourism growth with public health involves:

- **Health and Safety Protocols**: Implementing stringent health and safety protocols in tourism destinations, including regular sanitation, social distancing measures, and health screenings. These measures ensure that both tourists and residents feel safe, which is crucial for restoring confidence in travel. For example, enhanced cleaning procedures in hotels, mandatory mask-wearing in crowded places, and frequent sanitization of public transport can significantly reduce the risk of disease transmission.
- **Vaccination Campaigns**: Promoting and facilitating vaccination campaigns for both residents and travelers to ensure a safe and healthy environment. This includes providing easy access to vaccines, running awareness programs about the benefits of vaccination, and possibly requiring proof of vaccination for entry into certain destinations or participation in specific activities.
- **Public Health Infrastructure**: Strengthening public health infrastructure in tourism hotspots to handle potential outbreaks and ensure the safety of both tourists and local communities. This involves increasing healthcare capacity, such as hospitals and clinics, training healthcare workers, and ensuring the availability of necessary medical supplies and equipment.

Sustainable Growth

Sustainable tourism growth requires balancing economic benefits with environmental and social considerations:

- **Carrying Capacity**: Assessing and managing the carrying capacity of tourism destinations to prevent over-tourism and its negative impacts on local ecosystems and communities. Carrying capacity studies help determine the maximum number of visitors that an area can accommodate without causing significant harm. For instance, implementing visitor quotas or seasonal restrictions can help manage tourist influx and protect sensitive environments.

- **Economic Diversification**: Encouraging economic diversification in tourism-dependent regions to reduce vulnerability to future crises and promote long-term sustainability. This might involve developing alternative income sources such as agriculture, crafts, or technology sectors, thereby reducing reliance on tourism alone. Diversification makes local economies more resilient to shocks like pandemics or natural disasters.
- **Stakeholder Engagement**: Engaging local communities, businesses, and governments in tourism planning and decision-making to ensure inclusive and sustainable growth. Stakeholder engagement ensures that tourism development aligns with the needs and aspirations of local populations, leading to more equitable and sustainable outcomes. Collaborative platforms and forums can facilitate dialogue and shared decision-making among diverse stakeholders.

17.1.2 Implementing Sustainable Practices
Environmental Sustainability

Environmental sustainability is a cornerstone of sustainable tourism post-pandemic:

- **Conservation Efforts**: Promoting conservation efforts to protect natural resources and biodiversity in tourism destinations. This includes supporting protected areas, wildlife sanctuaries, and marine reserves. Conservation initiatives can involve local communities, providing them with incentives to protect and manage their natural resources sustainably.
- **Sustainable Infrastructure**: Developing and maintaining sustainable infrastructure, such as eco-friendly accommodations, renewable energy sources, and efficient waste management systems. Sustainable buildings, for example, use energy-efficient technologies, minimize water use, and incorporate renewable energy sources like solar or wind power.

- **Carbon Footprint Reduction**: Implementing measures to reduce the carbon footprint of tourism activities, including promoting low-emission transportation options and encouraging carbon offset programs. Initiatives such as electric vehicle use, biking and walking tours, and carbon offsetting for flights can significantly reduce the environmental impact of travel.

Social and Cultural Sustainability

Social and cultural sustainability is equally important in balancing tourism growth and public health:

- **Cultural Preservation**: Supporting initiatives that preserve and promote local cultures, traditions, and heritage sites. This includes involving local communities in tourism activities and respecting cultural sensitivities. Cultural preservation efforts can include funding for cultural events, restoration projects for historical sites, and educational programs about local heritage.
- **Community Empowerment**: Empowering local communities through tourism by creating job opportunities, supporting local businesses, and ensuring fair distribution of economic benefits. Empowerment can take the form of training programs, microfinance initiatives for small businesses, and policies that prioritize local hiring and sourcing.
- **Health and Well-being**: Prioritizing the health and well-being of both tourists and local residents by ensuring access to healthcare, promoting mental health initiatives, and fostering a safe and inclusive environment. Well-being initiatives can include wellness tourism programs, stress-relief activities, and ensuring healthcare facilities are accessible and affordable.

17.2 Community-Based Tourism
17.2.1 Benefits of Community-Based Tourism
Economic Benefits

Community-based tourism (CBT) offers significant economic benefits for local communities:

- **Local Employment**: CBT creates job opportunities for local residents, reducing unemployment rates and boosting local economies. Jobs can range from tour guides and hospitality staff to artisans and transportation providers.
- **Income Generation**: CBT provides additional income streams for local communities through tourism-related activities such as guiding, hospitality services, and the sale of local products. This diversification of income sources can enhance economic resilience.
- **Economic Diversification**: CBT helps diversify local economies by reducing dependence on traditional industries and promoting sustainable economic development. By leveraging tourism, communities can create new markets for local products and services.

Social and Cultural Benefits

CBT also promotes social and cultural benefits:

- **Cultural Exchange**: CBT fosters cultural exchange between tourists and local communities, promoting mutual understanding and appreciation of different cultures. This exchange can enhance cultural pride and identity among local residents while providing tourists with authentic and enriching experiences.
- **Community Empowerment**: CBT empowers local communities by involving them in tourism planning and decision-making processes, ensuring that tourism development aligns with their needs and aspirations. Empowerment initiatives can include participatory planning workshops and the establishment of community tourism boards.
- **Preservation of Traditions**: CBT supports the preservation of local traditions, crafts, and heritage, providing incentives for communities to maintain their cultural practices. By making cultural heritage an integral part of the tourism experience, CBT ensures that these traditions remain vibrant and relevant.

17.2.2 Implementing Community-Based Tourism
Community Involvement

Successful CBT initiatives require active community involvement:

- **Participatory Planning**: Engaging local communities in the planning and development of tourism projects ensures that their voices are heard and their needs are addressed. Participatory approaches can include community meetings, surveys, and collaborative workshops.
- **Capacity Building**: Providing training and capacity-building programs for local residents equips them with the skills and knowledge needed to participate in and benefit from tourism activities. Training can cover areas such as hospitality management, language skills, marketing, and sustainable practices.
- **Collaborative Partnerships**: Establishing collaborative partnerships between local communities, governments, NGOs, and the private sector fosters a supportive environment for CBT. Partnerships can facilitate resource sharing, technical support, and joint marketing efforts.

Sustainable Practices

CBT should adhere to sustainable practices to ensure long-term success:

- **Environmental Stewardship**: Encouraging environmental stewardship among local communities by promoting conservation efforts and sustainable resource management practices. This can involve community-led initiatives to protect local ecosystems and biodiversity.
- **Cultural Sensitivity**: Ensuring that tourism activities respect and preserve local cultures and traditions, avoiding cultural commodification and exploitation. Cultural sensitivity training for tourists and service providers can help maintain the integrity

of cultural heritage.

- **Fair Distribution of Benefits**: Implementing mechanisms to ensure the fair distribution of economic benefits from tourism activities, prioritizing the well-being of local communities. Benefit-sharing models can include community funds, profit-sharing schemes, and direct financial support for community projects.

17.3 Eco-Friendly Certifications
17.3.1 Role of Eco-Friendly Certifications
Guiding Sustainable Choices

Eco-friendly certifications play a crucial role in guiding travelers towards sustainable choices:

- **Trust and Credibility**: Eco-friendly certifications provide travelers with assurance that certified businesses and destinations adhere to recognized sustainability standards. Certifications from reputable organizations signal a commitment to high environmental and social standards.
- **Informed Decision-Making**: Eco-friendly certifications enable travelers to make informed decisions by highlighting environmentally responsible options for accommodations, tours, and activities. Certified options often feature prominently in eco-conscious travel guides and booking platforms.
- **Market Differentiation**: Eco-friendly certifications help businesses differentiate themselves in the market by showcasing their commitment to sustainability, attracting eco-conscious travelers. This differentiation can lead to increased market share and customer loyalty.

Promoting Sustainable Practices

Eco-friendly certifications encourage the adoption of sustainable practices:

- **Environmental Standards**: Certified businesses must meet stringent environmental standards, including energy and water conservation, waste reduction, and sustainable sourcing of materials. These standards help minimize the environmental impact of tourism operations.
- **Social Responsibility**: Eco-friendly certifications often include criteria related to social responsibility, such as fair labor practices, community engagement, and cultural preservation. These criteria ensure that tourism benefits local communities and respects their rights and heritage.
- **Continuous Improvement**: Certification programs encourage continuous improvement by requiring businesses to regularly review and enhance their sustainability practices. Regular audits and updates to certification criteria help businesses stay aligned with evolving best practices.

17.3.2 Types of Eco-Friendly Certifications

Global and Regional Certifications

Several global and regional eco-friendly certifications guide sustainable tourism:

- **Global Sustainable Tourism Council (GSTC)**: The GSTC provides global standards for sustainable tourism, offering certification programs for accommodations, tour operators, and destinations. GSTC certification ensures compliance with comprehensive sustainability criteria covering environmental, social, and economic aspects.
- **Green Key**: Green Key is an international eco-label for tourism facilities, promoting environmental awareness and sustainable practices in the hospitality industry. Green Key-certified establishments must meet rigorous criteria related to environmental management and sustainability education.
- **Blue Flag**: The Blue Flag certification recognizes sustainable beach and marina management, promoting clean and safe coastal environments. Blue Flag awards are based on strict

criteria for water quality, environmental education, safety, and services.

Sector-Specific Certifications

Sector-specific certifications address sustainability in different tourism sectors:

- **LEED Certification**: LEED (Leadership in Energy and Environmental Design) certification recognizes sustainable building practices in the construction and operation of hotels and other tourism facilities. LEED certification emphasizes energy efficiency, water conservation, and sustainable site development.
- **Travelife**: Travelife certification focuses on sustainability in the travel and tourism industry, providing guidelines for tour operators, travel agencies, and accommodations. Travelife-certified businesses must demonstrate commitments to environmental protection, fair labor practices, and community engagement.
- **Rainforest Alliance**: The Rainforest Alliance certification promotes sustainable tourism practices in biodiversity-rich areas, supporting conservation and community development. Certified businesses must adhere to rigorous standards that protect ecosystems and promote the well-being of local communities.

17.4 Promoting Eco-friendly and Responsible Travel
17.4.1 Educating Travelers
Raising Awareness

Educating travelers about eco-friendly and responsible travel is essential:

- **Awareness Campaigns**: Implementing awareness campaigns to inform travelers about the environmental and social impacts of their travel choices and encourage responsible behavior.

Campaigns can use various media, including social media, websites, and informational brochures.

- **Sustainability Guidelines**: Providing sustainability guidelines and tips for travelers, including advice on reducing carbon footprints, conserving resources, and respecting local cultures. These guidelines can be distributed through travel agencies, online platforms, and at tourist information centers.
- **Interactive Workshops**: Organizing interactive workshops and seminars on sustainable travel practices, engaging travelers in discussions and activities that promote eco-friendly behaviors. Workshops can cover topics such as zero-waste travel, ethical wildlife tourism, and carbon offsetting.

Encouraging Responsible Behavior

Encouraging responsible behavior among travelers involves:

- **Eco-Friendly Practices**: Promoting eco-friendly practices such as using reusable water bottles, minimizing plastic use, and supporting local businesses and products. Travelers can be encouraged to reduce waste, use public transportation, and choose eco-certified accommodations.
- **Respecting Local Communities**: Encouraging travelers to respect local communities by adhering to cultural norms, supporting community-based tourism initiatives, and engaging in volunteer activities. Respectful behavior includes learning about and observing local customs and traditions.
- **Wildlife Conservation**: Educating travelers about the importance of wildlife conservation and promoting responsible wildlife tourism practices that do not harm animals or their habitats. This includes discouraging activities that exploit or endanger wildlife, such as unethical animal encounters or buying products made from endangered species.

17.4.2 Sustainable Travel Trends
Slow Travel

Slow travel is a growing trend that emphasizes quality over quantity:

- **Extended Stays**: Slow travel encourages extended stays in destinations, allowing travelers to immerse themselves in local cultures and communities. Longer stays can reduce the environmental impact of frequent travel and provide more meaningful experiences.
- **Reduced Carbon Footprint**: By traveling less frequently and spending more time in each destination, slow travel reduces the overall carbon footprint of travel. This approach often involves choosing more sustainable modes of transport, such as trains or buses, and focusing on local exploration.
- **Authentic Experiences**: Slow travel prioritizes authentic experiences and meaningful interactions with local people, fostering a deeper understanding of destinations. Travelers may participate in local activities, learn traditional crafts, and engage in community events.

Eco-Tourism

Eco-tourism focuses on sustainable and nature-based travel experiences:

- **Nature Conservation**: Eco-tourism promotes the conservation of natural environments and biodiversity by supporting protected areas and conservation projects. Eco-tourists often visit national parks, wildlife reserves, and other natural sites where their presence can contribute to conservation funding.
- **Educational Experiences**: Eco-tourism offers educational experiences that raise awareness about environmental issues and promote sustainable practices. Guided nature walks, wildlife safaris, and eco-lodges often include educational components that teach visitors about local ecosystems and conservation efforts.

- **Community Benefits**: Eco-tourism ensures that local communities benefit economically and socially from tourism activities, supporting livelihoods and cultural preservation. Eco-tourism initiatives can provide direct financial benefits to communities through employment, revenue-sharing, and support for local businesses.

Sustainable tourism post-pandemic represents a paradigm shift towards a more responsible and environmentally conscious approach to travel. Balancing tourism growth with public health, promoting community-based tourism, implementing eco-friendly certifications, and encouraging eco-friendly and responsible travel practices are essential components of this transformation. By adopting sustainable practices and fostering collaboration among stakeholders, the tourism industry can build resilience, protect natural and cultural resources, and ensure a sustainable future for travel. The lessons learned from the pandemic offer an unprecedented opportunity to reshape the tourism industry into a force for good, fostering a harmonious relationship between travelers, destinations, and the planet.

CHAPTER EIGHTEEN

CONCLUSION AND FUTURE DIRECTIONS

18.1 Summarizing Key Findings

The intersection of communicable diseases and the tourism industry has been profoundly impactful, as seen through the various pandemics and outbreaks that have shaped global travel over the decades. This book has explored these impacts in depth, highlighting the following key findings:

18.1.1 Historical Impacts of Pandemics

- **HIV/AIDS and Modern Tourism**: The HIV/AIDS pandemic changed public perception of health risks associated with travel and led to significant modifications in the tourism industry's approach to health and safety.
- **SARS and the Early 2000s**: The SARS outbreak underscored the rapid spread of infectious diseases through international travel, prompting improved global health alert systems and stringent public health measures.
- **H1N1 Influenza (Swine Flu)**: The H1N1 pandemic emphasized the need for rapid response and adaptable public health strategies to mitigate the economic and social impacts on tourism.
- **Ebola Outbreak**: The Ebola crisis highlighted the severe effects on regional tourism and the role of media coverage in shaping

public perception and travel behavior.

18.1.2 Industry Adaptations and Innovations

- **Hygiene Protocols and Safety Measures**: The industry has implemented comprehensive hygiene protocols to ensure traveler safety and rebuild confidence.
- **Sustainability Initiatives**: The pandemic accelerated the adoption of sustainability initiatives, promoting eco-friendly and responsible travel practices.
- **Contact Tracing and Health Passports**: Digital tools like contact tracing apps and health passports have become crucial in managing health risks and facilitating safe travel.
- **Digital Transformation and Contactless Travel**: The shift towards digital solutions and contactless services has enhanced travel convenience and safety.

18.1.3 Marketing and Communication Strategies

- **Crisis Management**: Effective crisis management and communication are vital in addressing the challenges posed by pandemics and ensuring industry resilience.
- **Traveler Assurance**: Providing clear and transparent information about safety measures has been essential in reassuring travelers and encouraging safe travel practices.
- **Leveraging Social Media**: Social media has played a pivotal role in disseminating information, rebuilding traveler confidence, and promoting safe destinations.

18.1.4 Building Resilience in the Tourism Industry

- **Lessons Learned from Past Outbreaks**: The industry has gleaned valuable lessons from past pandemics, emphasizing the importance of preparedness and adaptability.

- **Cross-Sector Collaboration**: Collaboration between the tourism industry and public health sectors is crucial in managing health crises and ensuring a coordinated response.
- **Scenario Planning**: Scenario planning and simulations help prepare for future outbreaks and enhance the industry's capacity to respond effectively.
- **Strategies for Future Preparedness**: Developing robust strategies for future preparedness ensures that the industry can withstand and recover from health emergencies.

18.1.5 The Role of Technology in Future Travel

- **Predictive Analytics and Health Monitoring**: Advanced technologies like predictive analytics and health monitoring systems are essential in managing travel health risks.
- **Innovations in Travel Technology**: Ongoing innovations in travel technology, including AI and biometric solutions, are transforming the travel experience and enhancing security.
- **Artificial Intelligence and Predictive Analytics**: AI and predictive analytics offer significant potential in anticipating health risks and optimizing travel safety measures.
- **Biometric Technology**: Biometric technology enhances travel security and efficiency, facilitating seamless and safe travel experiences.

18.1.6 Sustainable Tourism Post-Pandemic

- **Balancing Tourism Growth and Public Health**: Achieving a balance between tourism growth and public health is crucial for long-term sustainability.
- **Community-Based Tourism**: Community-based tourism promotes sustainability by empowering local communities and preserving cultural heritage.
- **Eco-Friendly Certifications**: Eco-friendly certifications guide travelers towards sustainable choices and encourage

environmentally responsible practices.

- **Promoting Eco-friendly and Responsible Travel**: Educating travelers about eco-friendly and responsible travel practices is essential in fostering a sustainable tourism industry.

18.2 Future Research Directions
18.2.1 Understanding Long-Term Impacts

- **Economic Impact Analysis**: Conducting in-depth studies on the long-term economic impacts of pandemics on different segments of the tourism industry.
- **Behavioral Changes in Travelers**: Investigating how pandemics influence traveler behavior, preferences, and decision-making processes in the long term.
- **Health and Safety Protocols**: Assessing the effectiveness of various health and safety protocols implemented during pandemics and their impact on traveler confidence.

18.2.2 Technological Innovations

- **AI and Machine Learning**: Exploring the potential of AI and machine learning in predicting and managing health risks in travel.
- **Blockchain for Health Passports**: Evaluating the use of blockchain technology for secure and efficient health passports and vaccination records.
- **Virtual and Augmented Reality**: Studying the impact of virtual and augmented reality on tourism marketing and traveler engagement.

18.2.3 Sustainable Tourism Practices

- **Impact of Eco-Friendly Certifications**: Assessing the effectiveness of eco-friendly certifications in promoting sustainable travel behaviors and their impact on the environment.

- **Community Resilience**: Investigating the role of community-based tourism in enhancing community resilience and economic sustainability.
- **Climate Change Adaptation**: Studying the impact of climate change on tourism destinations and developing strategies for adaptation and mitigation.

18.2.4 Cross-Sector Collaboration

- **Public-Private Partnerships**: Examining the effectiveness of public-private partnerships in managing health crises and promoting sustainable tourism.
- **Global Health Governance**: Investigating the role of global health governance in coordinating international responses to pandemics and supporting the tourism industry.

18.3 Call to Action
18.3.1 For Policymakers

- **Strengthen Health Infrastructure**: Invest in strengthening health infrastructure in tourism destinations to ensure preparedness for future health crises.
- **Promote Sustainable Policies**: Implement policies that promote sustainable tourism practices and encourage eco-friendly initiatives.
- **Facilitate Collaboration**: Foster collaboration between the tourism industry, public health sectors, and other stakeholders to ensure a coordinated response to health emergencies.

18.3.2 For Industry Leaders

- **Adopt Best Practices**: Embrace best practices in crisis management, health and safety protocols, and sustainability to build resilience in the tourism industry.

- **Leverage Technology**: Invest in technological innovations that enhance travel safety, efficiency, and sustainability.
- **Engage Communities**: Engage local communities in tourism planning and decision-making to ensure that tourism development aligns with their needs and aspirations.

18.3.3 For Travelers

- **Practice Responsible Travel**: Adopt responsible travel behaviors, such as supporting local businesses, respecting cultural norms, and minimizing environmental impact.
- **Stay Informed**: Stay informed about health risks and safety measures in travel destinations and adhere to recommended guidelines.
- **Support Sustainable Tourism**: Choose eco-friendly and sustainable travel options, and encourage others to do the same.

18.4 Final Thoughts on the Future of Travel and Tourism

The future of travel and tourism will be shaped by the lessons learned from past pandemics and the ongoing commitment to resilience, sustainability, and innovation. The industry must continue to evolve, adopting best practices and embracing new technologies to ensure the safety and well-being of travelers and local communities. By fostering collaboration, promoting sustainable tourism practices, and leveraging technological advancements, the tourism industry can build a more resilient and sustainable future.

The journey ahead will undoubtedly present challenges, but with a shared commitment to responsible and sustainable travel, the tourism industry can emerge stronger and more resilient. The experiences and insights gained from navigating past pandemics will serve as a foundation for building a vibrant and sustainable tourism industry that can withstand future crises and continue to inspire and connect people around the world.